Library Management of Disciplinary Repositories

SPEC KITS

Supporting Effective Library Management for Over 40 Years

Committed to assisting research and academic libraries in the continuous improvement of management systems, ARL has worked since 1970 to gather and disseminate the best practices for library needs. As part of its commitment, ARL maintains an active publications program best known for its SPEC Kits. Through the Collaborative Research/Writing Program, librarians work with ARL staff to design SPEC surveys and write publications. Originally established as an information source for ARL member libraries, the SPEC Kit series has grown to serve the needs of the library community worldwide.

What are SPEC Kits?

Published six times per year, SPEC Kits contain the most valuable, up-to-date information on the latest issues of concern to libraries and librarians today. They are the result of a systematic survey of ARL member libraries on a particular topic related to current practice in the field. Each SPEC Kit contains an executive summary of the survey results; survey questions with tallies and selected comments; the best representative documents from survey participants, such as policies, procedures, handbooks, guidelines, Web sites, records, brochures, and statements; and a selected reading list—both print and online sources—containing the most current literature available on the topic for further study.

Subscribe to SPEC Kits

Subscribers tell us that the information contained in SPEC Kits is valuable to a variety of users, both inside and outside the library. SPEC Kit purchasers use the documentation found in SPEC Kits as a point of departure for research and problem solving because they lend immediate authority to proposals and set standards for designing programs or writing procedure statements. SPEC Kits also function as an important reference tool for library administrators, staff, students, and professionals in allied disciplines who may not have access to this kind of information.

SPEC Kits are available in print and online. The executive summary for each kit after December 1993 can be accessed online free of charge. For more information visit: **http://www.arl.org/publications-resources**.

SPEC Kit 338

Library Management of Disciplinary Repositories
November 2013

Jessica Adamick and Rachel Lewellen

University of Massachusetts Amherst

Rebecca Reznik-Zellen

University of Massachusetts Medical School

ASSOCIATION OF RESEARCH LIBRARIES

Series Editor: Lee Anne George

SPEC Kits are published by the

Association of Research Libraries
21 Dupont Circle, NW, Suite 800
Washington, DC 20036-1118
P (202) 296-2296 F (202) 872-0884
http://www.arl.org/publications-resources
pubs@arl.org

ISSN 0160 3582
ISBN 1-59407-909-9 / 978-1-59407-909-2 print
ISBN 1-59407-910-2 / 978-1-59407-910-8 online

Copyright © 2013

 The paper used in this publication meets the requirements of ANSI/NISO Z39.48-1992 (R1997) Permanence of Paper for Publications and Documents in Libraries and Archives.

SPEC
Kit 338

Library Management of Disciplinary Repositories

November 2013

SURVEY RESULTS

REPRESENTATIVE DOCUMENTS

tDAR

MHHE Archive

SELECTED RESOURCES

SURVEY RESULTS

EXECUTIVE SUMMARY

Introduction

Disciplinary repositories are open access, host scholarly materials,[1] accept deposits from national or international contributors, and are disciplinary, multidisciplinary, or interdisciplinary resources. They are a significant component of the scholarly communication environment, and can be highly visible and important mechanisms for sharing disciplinary research to dedicated communities. This survey was developed to gain a better understanding of the ways in which research libraries are involved in the administration of disciplinary repositories. It was distributed to the 125 ARL member libraries in July 2013 and these results are based on data submitted by 49 libraries (39%) by the deadline of September 3, 2013.

Thirteen respondents reported that their institution hosts or manages a disciplinary repository. The survey identified 34 disciplinary repositories managed by ARL institutions, both with and without library involvement. For the purposes of this study, the 12 repositories that are managed entirely or in part by the library are analyzed.[2] The 12 repositories are based at seven ARL institutions, which comprise 6% of ARL membership, demonstrating that disciplinary repository management is not widespread among ARL membership. While most respondents reported management of a single repository, two institutions manage many repositories. The University of Pittsburgh Libraries manage six disciplinary repositories in partnership with other campus departments or other institutions. At Purdue University, the Libraries manage one disciplinary repository, and other campus departments manage 16 disciplinary repositories.

The development and management of disciplinary repositories seem to be unique to local circumstances,

and disciplinary repositories are certainly not as common as institutional repositories. Institutional repositories are nearly always based in an institution's library, but disciplinary repositories have several models of management, only some of which involve a library. Some disciplinary repositories are managed solely by the library. Others use a library partnership with a parent institution department, a library partnership with a non-parent institution, a department as sole manager, multiple departmental partnerships, or multiple institution partnerships. Diverse management models may be a contributing factor to the lack of information published about disciplinary repository management (Adamick and Reznik-Zellen 2010).

Library management of disciplinary repositories supports one of ARL's basic principles that "Research libraries are active agents central to the process of the transmission and creation of knowledge" (Association of Research Libraries). A repository itself can help to document and define an area of study by collecting disparate research and making it discoverable in one place. The library can bring significant added value to a disciplinary repository, for example, through the development of a controlled vocabulary. Eight of the twelve repositories have developed a controlled vocabulary, which can help to define and document disciplinary terminology. Preservation is another value that libraries add to disciplinary repositories, although in most cases it was not a reported driving factor for repository development.

Like institutional repositories, disciplinary repositories require substantial staff mediation, quality control, and outreach efforts to build and maintain their specialized collections. Low contribution rates reported by a few of the respondents indicate that the disconnect between curation activities and the research cycle (Pryor 2012) presents a barrier even for publication-oriented disciplinary repositories. The obvious exception to this is PubMed Central®, which alone has the benefit of federal legislation for content deposit. Dedicated services for knowledge generation facilitate the success of subject repositories (Armbruster and Romary 2009), and many repositories in this survey provide social networking and community building tools as well as content to their communities.

Disciplinary repositories are also similar to institutional repositories in that they both require a significant financial investment to operate. A variety of funding mechanisms, including external grant funding, internal library budgets, one-time supplements, endowments, and membership fees are employed alone or in combination to support these initiatives. Many repositories included in this study use unique funding models, but more than half of the reporting libraries support their disciplinary repositories through their own budgets. This support may contribute to a sense of confidence in repository sustainability.

There were few meaningful trends identified in the survey responses, and the low number of library-managed repositories identified are best presented in a case study report format. Because of their explicit focus on specialized communities and diverse management models, the lack of identifiable trends seems appropriate. Although disciplinary communities have a common dedication to broadening access to their research outputs, they assemble a variety of administrative models, collection development strategies, and outreach mechanisms to accomplish their goals.

Origins, Subjects, and Communities

While there are many reasons that a community would undertake the effort of developing a disciplinary repository, the primary reason reported is a desire to alleviate the barriers of accessing the literature and other resources within the discipline (see Figure 1). Centralizing resources and increasing their visibility support this inclination to remove barriers to access. The Aphasiology Archive, for example, explicitly noted the need to create a central location for the products of an annual disciplinary conference. A call from the disciplinary community itself was frequently reported, as was some evidence of community readiness that a disciplinary resource was needed. In some cases, the opportunity to leverage a funding source, or

Figure 1: Motivating Factors for the Development of a Disciplinary Repository

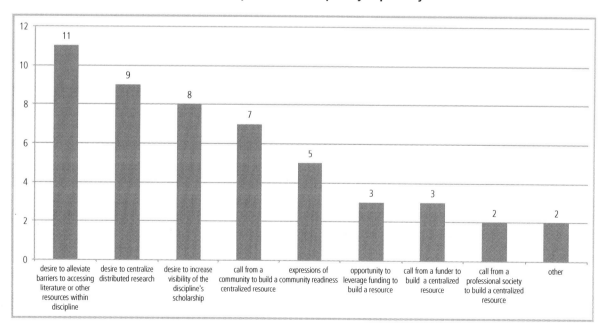

an explicit call from a funder were motivating factors. As an extension of this concept, InterNano noted that its development was part of "broader impacts" activities for a large research center, making it an important component of an overarching research project. Only one repository, Dryad, cited the need for preservation and archiving policies. PubMed Central, because of its unique status as the mandated repository for the National Institutes of Health (NIH), was developed out of a need to share the publicly funded products of the NIH research community. As noted by the respondent, "This initially voluntary activity was later mandated by Congress in 2008 through a requirement of National Institutes of Health researchers to submit final, peer-reviewed manuscripts to PubMed Central."

Of the 12 disciplinary repositories represented, the earliest was established in 1995 and the most recent was launched in 2013. Between 2000 and 2013, a repository was established almost annually, with the exception of 2005, 2006, and 2011 (see Table 1). However, none of the ARL libraries that responded to the survey reported active or future planning to launch a disciplinary repository.

As expected, disciplinary repositories are more common in the sciences, with only three social science repositories and two humanities repositories among those represented in this study. This may be due to the continued high rate of publication in the sciences, as well as the increase in scientific grey literature (Larsen and von Ins 2010).

The primary audience for disciplinary repositories is the academic communities that they serve. Government, non-profit workers, and industry professionals are other common audience segments, which is unsurprising given the subject matter of many of the repositories in this study. Students and the general public are less commonly reported as target audiences, although The Digital Archaeological Record (tDAR) noted, "The repository contents [are] not explicitly designed to be of interest to the general public, however, many of the visitors to the repository website appear to be members of the general public who have an interest in the archaeology of specific geographical areas or topics. We are pleased that the repository also is of interest to this audience and may in the future develop features that are of interest and relevance to such visitors and users." This is an unintended positive consequence of providing open access to disciplinary scholarly resources. Dryad uniquely includes publishers, learned societies, research institutions, and funding bodies as part of their primary audience. Dryad's content focus on research data and their content recruitment model of partnering with publishers may contribute to extended audiences.

Table 1. Repository Launch Date and Subject Coverage

Repository	Launch Date	Subject Coverage
AgEcon Search	1995	Agriculture and applied economics
PubMed Central®	2000	Biomedicine
HABRI Central	2012	Human-animal interaction
Industry Studies Working Papers	2010	Industry studies
InterNano	2007	Nanomanufacturing
The Aphasiology Archive	2003	Communication impairments and disorders
Dryad	2008	Evolutionary biology and ecology
PhilSci-Archive	2001	Philosophy of science
Resources in Integrated Care for Morbidity Management and Disability Prevention (RIIC-4MMDP)	2013	Neglected tropical diseases, disability prevention, early detection of disease and prevention
Archive of European Integration	2002	European integration
The Digital Archaeological Record (tDAR)	2009	Archaeology and related fields
Minority Health and Health Equity Archive	2004	Minority health, health disparities, ethnic and racial disparities in health research, policy, and services

Most repositories did not have a sense of audience size. Only four repositories were able to identify audience size, based on the size of the disciplinary research community, industry market, or government stakeholders. For InterNano, specifically, the range of audience types and sectors presented a barrier to gauging the size of the audience accurately. These responses indicate a need to develop a tool to gauge audience size for assessment purposes.

There are several reported preparatory activities performed prior to launching a disciplinary repository. The most common activity is the formation of an advisory board. Researching repository features, repository software, and the disciplinary environment, and creating a strategic plan for the repository are also common activities that inform repository development. HABRI Central solicited market and sustainability plans from consultants and literature reviews. Less common development activities are those that directly or indirectly solicit stakeholder feedback, such as workshops or charrettes, focus groups, or user or author surveys. Expense, time, and specialized skills required to successfully undertake these information-gathering and planning activities are considerations for disciplinary repository managers.

Features and Content

When asked about the software platform that the repositories are built upon, more than half of the respondents report using the United Kingdom-based EPrints[3] software. DSpace[4] is used by AgEcon Search and Dryad; HubZero[5] is used by HABRI Central; custom software platforms have been implemented by PubMed Central and tDAR. Dryad also incorporates custom software with their DSpace installation.

Apart from the research content that is provided by these repositories, respondents were asked about the other tools and resources that they offer to provide disciplinary context and develop community. Social networking and sharing tools are the most common, with reported ties to Twitter, Facebook, email discussion lists, RSS feeds, blogs, and LinkedIn. More labor-intensive electronic newsletters and calendars are also provided. InterNano provides a directory, original content, and a disciplinary technical process database to its users; HABRI Central offers simulation tools and statistical packages, as well as a discussion forum. PubMed Central is unique in that it is integrated with an established suite of bibliographic and database tools provided by the National Center for Biotechnology Information.[6]

All of the repositories promote use to their communities, mostly through conference presentations, email announcements, and newsletters. None of the repositories have a "build it and they will come" model, they instead use active marketing practices and make arrangements with organizations to build their collections. Repositories perform a number of content recruitment methods, and all of the repositories reported formal arrangements with publishers, professional organizations, research centers, or funding bodies to recruit content. Most of the repositories have a policy that anyone can create an account and submit materials, and a practice that the repository staff create content. Nearly all respondents reported that repository staff monitor submissions to ensure they are within a repository's scope.

When asked if the recent government mandates have impacted their repository's collection development, most respondents did not perceive a change, but others were positive or aware of the impact of government mandates. For example, PubMed Central responded that a "Congressional mandate requires NIH funded manuscripts to be deposited, which has enriched the PubMed Central database and increased its usage," and tDAR responded, "In both positive and negative ways recent government actions, including mandates, have affected tDAR's content development. On the negative side, the budget cuts required by federal government sequestration have slowed the rate at which federal agency offices have decided to use tDAR to manage the archaeological information for which they are responsible. On the positive side, the Administration's developing policy of "Open Gov" and improving access to federal scientific data, including archaeological data, has created an interest in considering by federal agency offices in using tDAR to provide for this required access."

Respondents reported a wide range of accepted content types. The most commonly accepted content is working papers, and about half of the respondents accept pre-prints, post-prints, book chapters, books, datasets, slides, video, dissertations, theses, and reports.

The repositories described in the survey are very diverse in size, ranging from 38 digital objects in Resources in Integrated Care for Morbidity Management and Disability Prevention (RIIC-4MMDP), which is under development, to 2.8 million digital objects in PubMed Central, which is one of the largest disciplinary repositories in existence (see Table 2). When reporting the entire collection size (total records), two repositories have collections under 1,000 records, three repositories have collections between 1,000 and 10,000 records, and four repositories have collections between 10,000 and 100,000 records. AgEcon Search and Industry Studies host only full text items. All but three repositories reported that they have records that link to external resources, and a significant portion of the collections in the tDAR and HABRI Central repositories are links to external resources. The definition of collection size varies with each repository, based on the focus on digital objects or metadata records.

Table 2. Number of Digital Objects and Metadata Records in Each Repository

Repository	Digital Objects	Metadata Records	Percent of Collection is Full Text
AgEcon Search	66,000	66,000	100%
PubMed Central®	2.8 million	over 2.8 million	-
HABRI Central	400	17,000	2%
Industry Studies Working Papers	130	130	100%
InterNano	1,003	1,859	54%
The Aphasiology Archive	1,450	1,734	84%
Dryad	3,823	11,077	35%
PhilSci-Archive	3,392	not reported	-
RIIC-4MMDP	38	not reported	-
Archive of European Integration	27,171	not reported	-
tDAR	24,163	390,000	6%
Minority Health and Health Equity Archive	1,000	2,550	39%

All of the case study repositories require that metadata records include, at a minimum, the elements title, creator, and date published. Only five require an identifier element; seven require a publisher element. Other metadata elements required by some of the repositories include: format, status, refereed, conference title, location, language, and funding/grant data, among others (see Table 3).

Table 3. Metadata Properties Required by Each Repository

Repository	Title	Creator	Identifier	Publisher	Date Published	Other Metadata Fields
AgEcon Search	X	X	X		X	
PubMed Central®	X	X		X	X	X
HABRI Central	X	X	X	X	X	
Industry Studies Working Papers	X	X			X	X
InterNano	X	X	X	X	X	X
The Aphasiology Archive	X	X		X	X	X
Dryad	X	X	X	X	X	X
PhilSci	X	X			X	
RIIC-4MMDP	X	X	X		X	X
Archive of European Integration	X	X			X	

Repository	Title	Creator	Identifier	Publisher	Date Published	Other Metadata Fields
tDAR	x	x		x	x	x
Minority Health and Health Equity Archive	x	x		x	x	

All of the case study repositories allow authors to submit descriptive metadata for repository content, and most of them rely on repository staff and student workers to submit descriptive metadata, and/or enhance or perform quality control of the records. Eight of the 12 repositories have developed a customized vocabulary, which can help to document a field and standardize terminology (see Table 4).

Table 4. Metadata Practices of Each Repository

Repository	Who Enters Metadata?	Metadata Records	Descriptive Tools	Standardized Vocabularies
AgEcon Search	Authors Student workers	66,000	Local or customized vocabularies, Uncontrolled vocabularies (i.e., user tags, author keywords)	
PubMed Central®	Authors	2.8 million	Standardized vocabularies (i.e., LCSH, MeSH, NanoParticle Ontology)	MeSH
HABRI Central	Authors Repository staff Student workers	17,000	Local or customized vocabularies	
Industry Studies Working Papers	Authors Repository staff	130	Uncontrolled vocabularies (i.e., user tags, author keywords)	
InterNano	Authors Repository staff Student workers	1,859	Local or customized vocabularies Uncontrolled vocabularies (i.e., user tags, author keywords)	
The Aphasiology Archive	Authors Repository staff Student workers	1,734	Uncontrolled vocabularies (i.e., user tags, author keywords)	
Dryad	Authors Repository staff Student workers	11,077	Standardized vocabularies Local or customized vocabularies Uncontrolled vocabularies	ITIS, HIVE, LCNAF, LCSH, MeSH, NBII, TGN, UBio
PhilSci-Archive	Authors Repository staff Student workers		Uncontrolled vocabularies (i.e., user tags, author keywords)	
RIIC-4MMDP	Authors Repository staff Student workers	38	Local or customized vocabularies	
Archive of European Integration	Authors Repository staff Student workers		Local or customized vocabularies Uncontrolled vocabularies (i.e., user tags, author keywords)	
tDAR	Authors Repository staff Student workers Third party	390,000	Local or customized vocabularies Uncontrolled vocabularies (i.e., user tags, author keywords)	

Repository	Who Enters Metadata?	Metadata Records	Descriptive Tools	Standardized Vocabularies
Minority Health and Health Equity Archive	Authors Repository staff Student workers	2,550	Local or customized vocabularies Uncontrolled vocabularies (i.e., user tags, author keywords)	

Administration and Staffing

Eight ARL libraries support a disciplinary repository in some way, and some support more than one (see Figure 2). The University of Pittsburgh Libraries, for example, support multiple disciplinary repositories under two different administration models. Most commonly, the library partners either with the parent institution or with another institution. It is much less common for repositories to be administered by the library independently; only PubMed Central and AgEcon Search are administered by the library alone.

Sustainability of funds for repositories and other digital resources is a theme in literature about digital libraries (Maron and Pickle 2013), but only one repository reported an unsustainable funding model. Confidence of sustainability is probably due to the fact that seven of the repositories reported parent institution or internal library regular budget funding. Two of the three remaining repositories with external grant funding had a second income stream, which may explain confidence in sustainability. Two repositories received funding from multiple external sources. Of the six repositories that reported the receipt of external grant funding, four received funding from federal sources, and of those, three received funding from the National Science Foundation (see Table 5).

Figure 2: Administration Models for Disciplinary Repositories

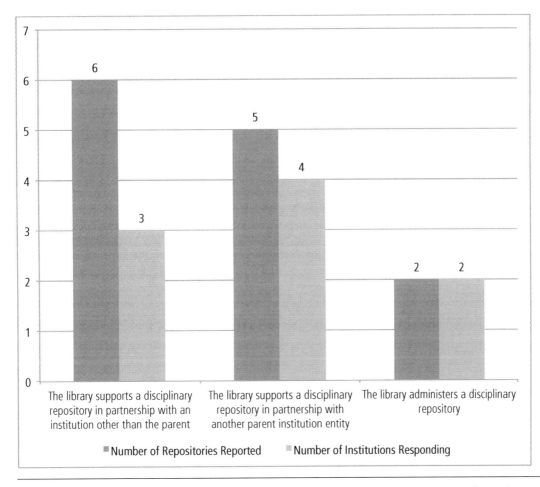

Table 5. Funding and Sustainability of Each Repository

Repository	Institution	Funding Model	External Grant Funding	Sustainable	Sustainability Plan	Budget
AgEcon Search	University of Minnesota	Internal library regular budget, One-time supplemental funds, Endowment fund, External grant funding	USDA National Agriculture Library, CME Foundation, Farm Foundation, AAEA Trust	Yes	No	102,000
PubMed Central®	National Library of Medicine	Parent institution budget		Yes	Yes	
HABRI Central	Purdue University	External grant funding	HABRI Foundation	Yes	Yes	350,000
Industry Studies Working Papers	University of Pittsburgh	Internal library regular budget		Yes	No	
InterNano	University of Massachusetts Amherst	External grant funding	National Science Foundation	No	In development	150,000
The Aphasiology Archive	University of Pittsburgh	Internal library regular budget		Yes	Yes	
Dryad	North Carolina State University	External grant funding, Membership fees, data publication charges, foundations, private donors	National Science Foundation	Yes	Yes	
PhilSci	University of Pittsburgh	Internal library regular budget		Yes	Yes	
RIIC-4MMDP	University of Pittsburgh	Internal library regular budget, External funding by non-profit partnership		Yes	No	
Archive of European Integration	University of Pittsburgh	Internal library regular budget		Yes	Yes	

Repository	Institution	Funding Model	External Grant Funding	Sustainable	Sustainability Plan	Budget
tDAR	Arizona State University	External grant funding, Contracts for digital archiving services and digital curation services	Andrew W. Mellon Foundation; National Science Foundation; National Endowment for the Humanities	Yes	Yes	800,000
Minority Health and Health Equity Archive	University of Pittsburgh	Internal library regular budget, External grant funding, Funding from the University of Maryland, separate from the University Library System, University of Pittsburgh funding		Yes	No	

In these repositories, staff sizes range from three to ten individuals representing 1.8 to 7.8 FTE. Staff positions are typically permanent, which may be related to the strong assertion that the funding models are believed to be sustainable. While many of the positions are full time, especially the project manager or director, it is unclear what percentage of those and other positions are dedicated exclusively to repository support.

Staff size does not seem related to collection size. The extent to which specialized subject knowledge is needed also varies.

Advisory boards seem to be an integral part of disciplinary repositories, involved with aspects of their development and administration. Nine of the 12 case study repositories have an advisory board, each with academic members, but the boards also include industry, government, and nonprofit representatives (see Figure 3). Seven of these boards were formed in the planning stages. Advisory boards are quite active, influencing the strategic direction, sustainability, outreach, policies, and collections activities of the repositories. However, they are not typically involved in the day-to-day workflows of the repositories (see Figure 4).

Figure 3: Advisory Board Member Composition

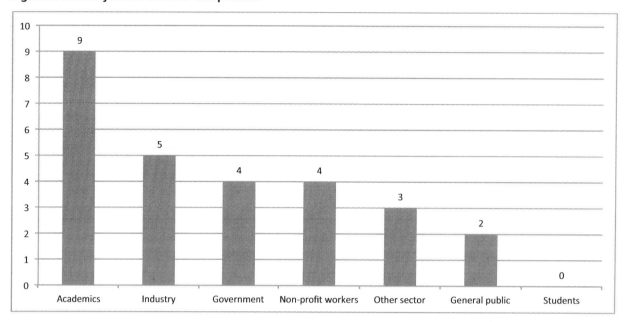

Figure 4: Influence of Advisory Board: 1 is no influence and 4 is large influence

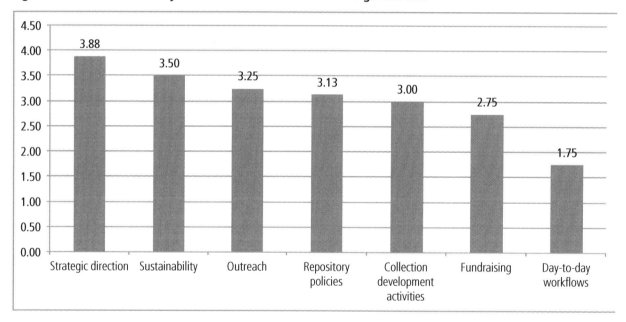

Of the seven case study institutions, four are assessing and two are planning to assess effectiveness. Web use statistics and download counts are the most widespread assessment techniques in use or being planned. User surveys, interviews, and focus groups have also been conducted (see Figure 5). One institution involved with six repositories does not plan to conduct assessment.

Figure 5: Assessment Methods

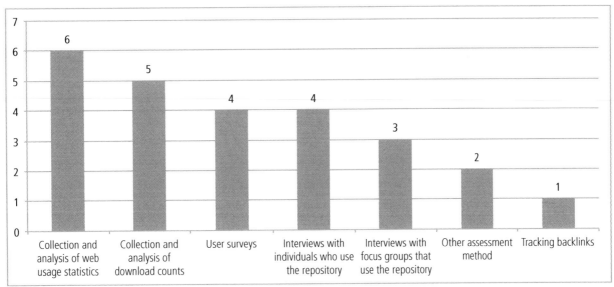

Conclusion

It is a challenge to identify common aspects of disciplinary repository management that can be abstracted from the particulars of their community focus and individual funding models. While disciplinary communities do hold in common a dedication to broadening access to their research outputs, they assemble a variety of administrative models, collection development strategies, and outreach mechanisms to accomplish their dissemination goals.

Library-Managed Repositories

Institution	Repository Name	Link
University of Minnesota	AgEcon Search	http://ageconsearch.umn.edu/
National Library of Medicine	PubMed Central®	http://www.ncbi.nlm.nih.gov/pmc/
Purdue University	HABRI Central	http://www.habricentral.org
University of Pittsburgh	Industry Studies Working Papers	http://isapapers.pitt.edu
University of Massachusetts Amherst	InterNano	http://www.internano.org/
University of Pittsburgh	The Aphasiology Archive	http://aphasiology.pitt.edu
Indiana University	Digital Library of the Commons	http://dlc.dlib.indiana.edu/dlc/
North Carolina State University	Dryad	https://datadryad.org/
University of Pittsburgh	PhilSci-Archive	http://philsci-archive.pitt.edu/
University of Pittsburgh	Resources in Integrated Care for Morbidity Management and Disability Prevention (RIIC-4MMDP)	http://www.riic4mmdp.org
University of Pittsburgh	Archive of European Integration	http://aei.pitt.edu/
Arizona State University	The Digital Archaeological Record (tDAR)	http://www.tdar.org/
University of Pittsburgh	Minority Health and Health Equity Archive	http://minority-health.pitt.edu

Repositories Identified through the Survey that are Based at ARL Institutions, but not Managed by the Library

Institution	Repository Name	Link
Pennsylvania State University	CiteSeerX	http://citeseerx.ist.psu.edu/index
Purdue University	C3Bio	http://c3bio.org/
Purdue University	CatalyzeCare	https://catalyzecare.org/
Purdue University	cceHUB	https://ccehub.org/
Purdue University	CLEERHub	http://cleerhub.org/
Purdue University	CUAHD	http://cuahd.org/
Purdue University	driNET	https://drinet.hubzero.org/
Purdue University	GEOSHARE	http://geoshareproject.org/
Purdue University	GlobalHUB	https://globalhub.org/
Purdue University	IASHub	http://isahub.com/
Purdue University	Indiana CTSI	https://www.indianactsi.org/
Purdue University	manufacturingHUB	http://manufacturinghub.org/
Purdue University	memsHUB	https://memshub.org/
Purdue University	nanoHUB	http://nanohub.org/
Purdue University	NEEShub	http://nees.org/
Purdue University	pharmaHUB	http://pharmahub.org/
Purdue University	STEMEdhub	http://stemedhub.org/
University of Connecticut	Global Cestode Database	http://tapewormdb.uconn.edu/
University of Connecticut	Trust-Hub	https://www.trust-hub.org/
University of Michigan	Inter-university Consortium for Political and Social Research (ICPSR)	http://www.icpsr.umich.edu/icpsrweb/landing.jsp
University of North Carolina at Chapel Hill	Dryad	http://datadryad.org/
York University	HTP Prints	http://htpprints.yorku.ca/

References

Adamick, Jessica, and Rebecca Reznik-Zellen. 2010. "Representation and Recognition of Subject Repositories." *D-Lib Magazine* 16, no. 9/10. Accessed December 2, 2013. doi:10.1045/september2010-adamick

Armbruster, Chris, and Laurent Romary. 2009. "Comparing Repository Types: Challenges and Barriers for Subject-Based Repositories, Research Repositories, National Repository Systems and Institutional Repositories in Serving Scholarly Communication." Accessed on December 2, 2013. http://dx.doi.org/10.2139/ssrn.1506905

Association of Research Libraries. "About." http://www.arl.org/about

Larsen, Peder Olesen, and Markus von Ins. 2010. "The Rate of Growth in Scientific Publication and the Decline in Coverage Provided by Science Citation Index." *Scientometrics* 84, no. 3: 575–603. Accessed on December 2, 2013. doi: 10.1007/s11192-010-0202-z

Maron, Nancy L, and Sarah Pickle. 2013. *Searching for Sustainability: Strategies from Eight Digitized Special Collections.* Washington, DC: Association of Research Libraries. http://www.arl.org/storage/documents/publications/searching-for-sustainability-report-nov2013.pdf

Pryor, Graham. 2012. *Managing Research Data.* Facet Publishing: London.

Endnotes

1   Scholarly materials may include materials such as pre-prints, post-prints, working papers, and data.

2   Indiana University (IU) identified the Digital Library of the Commons (DLC), to which their Libraries have provided technical support. IU did not complete the survey, so the DLC is not included as a case study.

3   http://www.eprints.org/us/

4   http://www.dspace.org/

5   http://hubzero.org/

6   https://www.ncbi.nlm.nih.gov/

This project was made possible in part by the Institute of Museum and Library Services grant number LG-51-12-0511-12.

INSTITUTE *of* **Museum**and**Library** SERVICES

SURVEY QUESTIONS AND RESPONSES

The SPEC Survey on Library Management of Disciplinary Repositories was designed by **Jessica Adamick**, Assistant to the Associate Director, and **Rachel Lewellen**, Assessment Librarian, at the University of Massachusetts Amherst; and **Rebecca Reznik-Zellen**, Head of Research and Scholarly Communication, University of Massachusetts Medical School Lamar Soutter Library. These results are based on data submitted by 49 of the 125 ARL member libraries (39%) by the deadline of September 3, 2013. The survey's introductory text and questions are reproduced below, followed by the response data and selected comments from the respondents.

Disciplinary or subject repositories—such as arXiv or AgEcon Search—play an important role in scholarly communication, by collecting and providing access to the research of a single subject or a set of related subjects. Some of the largest, oldest, and most prestigious repositories are disciplinary repositories and they are often cited as highly successful scholarly communication initiatives, particularly in relation to institutional repositories. There are hundreds of active disciplinary repositories worldwide, and they are poised to become even more prominent in North America given increased governmental interest in public access to the output of federally funded research. At the same time, disciplinary repositories are largely understudied; they are under-represented in library literature; and they are virtually absent from commonly used tools for repository development, management, and content acquisition (Adamick and Reznik-Zellen, 2010a).

A 2010 study of the ten largest disciplinary repositories found that eight of the ten repositories were hosted by a higher education institution, and four were hosted by university libraries (Adamick and Reznik-Zellen, 2010b). Research libraries are increasingly involved with the dissemination of scholarly output, but there are few broad-scoped studies on the management of disciplinary repositories from a library perspective.

The purpose of this survey is to better understand the management and development of disciplinary repositories. It explores the disciplinary scope of the repository, collection policies, funding models, assessment practices, and staffing, among other information.

For the purpose of this survey, a disciplinary repository:

- is open access,
- accepts deposits from national or international contributors,
- hosts scholarly materials (i.e., pre-prints, post-prints, reports, and working papers, or data),
- is a disciplinary, multidisciplinary, or interdisciplinary resource.

Institutional repositories, archives, and special collections are beyond the scope of this survey.

NOTE: Respondents whose libraries host a disciplinary repository will answer the majority of the questions. In those cases, this survey may take 30 minutes to complete. If your institution manages more than one disciplinary repository, please submit separate surveys to represent each one. You will need to use a different computer for each survey.

We thank you for your participation in this survey, which will be the first systematic look into the issue of library and university management of disciplinary repositories. Your participation will contribute to the formal documentation of the ways in which libraries and universities are contributing to the dissemination and management of disciplinary and interdisciplinary research on a national scale, demonstrating an impact beyond institutional walls.

BACKGROUND

Does your library/institution administer (host or manage)/support a disciplinary repository? N=55 [Note: There are multiple responses from some responding institutions.]

Yes, the library administers a disciplinary repository	2	4%
Yes, the library supports a disciplinary repository in partnership with another parent institution entity	5	9%
Yes, the library supports a disciplinary repository in partnership with an institution other than the parent	6	11%
Yes, our parent institution administers a disciplinary repository	6	11%
Not yet, but the library plans to administer a disciplinary repository	0	0%
No, and there are no plans to administer a disciplinary repository	36	65%

If the library administers a disciplinary repository, please identify the repository and specify the library department that is responsible for the repository. N=2

AgEcon Search http://ageconsearch.umn.edu/ administered by the University of Minnesota Libraries Research and Learning division in conjunction with the information technology staff.

PubMed Central (PMC) administered by the National Center for Biotechnology Information at the National Library of Medicine.

If the library supports a disciplinary repository in partnership with another parent institution entity, please identify the repository and specify the library and institution departments that are responsible for the repository. N=5

HABRI Central www.habricentral.org Publishing Services (Purdue University Press and Scholarly Publishing Services). HABRI Central, though administered by the library, involves a partnership with the College of Veterinary Medicine where the main PI, Dr. Alan M. Beck, is based.

Industry Studies Working Papers http://isapapers.pitt.edu/ in conjunction with the Industry Studies Association and the Katz School of Business, University of Pittsburgh

The University of Massachusetts Amherst manages InterNano. The Science and Engineering Library administers it with the Center for Hierarchical Manufacturing.

The Aphasiology Archive http://aphasiology.pitt.edu Department of Information Technology, University Library System, University of Pittsburgh AND Department of Communication Science and Disorders, School of Health and Rehabilitation Sciences, University of Pittsburgh

The Digital Library of the Commons http://dlc.dlib.indiana.edu/dlc/ is a collaborative project of the Vincent and Elinor Ostrom Workshop in Political Theory and Policy Analysis and the Indiana University Digital Library Program.

If the library supports a disciplinary repository in partnership with an institution other than the parent, please identify the repository and specify the other institution that is responsible for the repository. N=6

Dryad is hosted at North Carolina State University and administered by NESCent, a collaboration between Duke, University of North Carolina, and NCSU and funded by the NSF.

PhilSci-Archive is supported by the University Library System and Department of Philosophy of Science at the University of Pittsburgh, and the Philosophy of Science Association.

Resources in Integrated Care for Morbidity Management and Disability Prevention (RIIC-4MMDP) http://www.riic4mmdp.org is supported by the University Library System at the University of Pittsburgh and the American Leprosy Missions. This repository originally began as the Archive for Essential Limb Care http://www.archive4limbcare.org, a repository developed in conjunction with the University of Pittsburgh's School of Health and Rehabilitation Sciences. The new repository is currently under development.

The Archive of European Integration is supported by the University Library System and the University Center for International Studies at the University of Pittsburgh, and the European Research Papers Archive, European Union Center, and European Union Studies Association.

The Digital Archaeological Record (tDAR). tDAR is administered and managed by the Center for Digital Antiquity, which is located in the School of Human Evolution and Social Change (SHESC) at Arizona State University. The Center and SHESC are partners with the ASU Libraries in maintaining tDAR. The Center is physically located in the main library building, Hayden Library, on the Tempe campus of ASU.

The Minority Health and Health Equity Archive is managed by the Department of Information Technology in the University Library System at the University of Pittsburgh, and The Maryland Center for Health Equity in the School of Public Health at the University of Maryland College Park.

If your parent institution administers a disciplinary repository, please identify the repository and specify the department(s) or entity that is responsible for the repository. N=6

CiteSeerX is maintained by a research team led by Lee Giles, David Reese Professor at the College of Information Sciences and Technology, Penn State University.

Dryad http://datadryad.org/ is administered by the University of North Carolina at Chapel Hill. Faculty members in the School of Information and Library Science and the Department of Biology are co-PIs on this multi-institutional project. Duke and North Carolina State University also support this project.

HTP Prints http://htpprints.yorku.ca/ is edited and administered by Christopher D. Green of the History & Theory of Psychology Program at York University, and it is supported by the technical assistance of York University's Faculty of Arts Academic Technology Services.

Inter-university Consortium for Political and Social Research (ICPSR) is a unit within the Institute for Social Research at the University of Michigan and maintains its office in Ann Arbor, Michigan.

Purdue University administers a number of disciplinary repositories. nanoHUB and manufacturingHUB are administered by the Network for Computational Nanotechnology; NEES, Indiana CTSI, PharmaHUB, GlobalHUB, cceHUB, CUAHD,

STEMEdHUB, and drinet are administered by Discovery Park; memsHUB is administered by the NNSA Center of Prediction of Reliability, Integrity, and Survivability of Microsystems (PRISM); CLEERHub is administered by Engineering Education; CatalyzeCare is administered by the Regenstrief Center for Healthcare Engineering; C3Bio is administered by the Bindley Bioscience Center; IASHub is administered by the Institute for Accessible Science; and GEOSHARE is administered by the Burton D. Morgan Center for Entrepreneurship.

The University of Connecticut administers two disciplinary repositories. The Global Cestode Database http://tapewormdb.uconn.edu, http://tapeworms.uconn.edu/ is administered by Professor Janine N. Caira, Department of Ecology & Evolutionary Biology, and the University Information Technology Services at the University of Connecticut. The trust-HUB hardware security repository (https://www.trust-hub.org/about) is managed by Mark Tehranipoor at UConn (with support from the School of Engineering IT) and team members at Polytechnic Institute of NYU, Rice University, and University of California Los Angeles.

If you answered that the library administers/supports a disciplinary repository above, when you click the Next>> button below you will skip to the section on Repository Description.

If you answered that the library plans to administer a repository, you will skip to the section on Future Plans for a Disciplinary Repository.

If you answered either that your parent institution administers a repository or that there are no plans to administer a repository, you will exit the survey.

The following are case studies of each of the 12 library-administered or -supported repositories. [Note: Indiana did not complete the rest of the survey so the Digital Library of the Commons is not included in the case studies.]

AGECON SEARCH REPOSITORY DESCRIPTION

Please enter a brief description of the disciplinary repository.

AgEcon Search http://ageconsearch.umn.edu/ is a free-to-user Web resource with full-text of working papers, conference papers and journal articles in agricultural, development, energy, environmental, resource and other areas of applied economics. It is housed at the University of Minnesota, and co-sponsored by the Agricultural and Applied Economics Association (AAEA). Over 250 institutions contribute their material to AgEcon Search, and its 65,000+ papers receive over 300,000 downloads per month. Papers submitted to AgEcon Search also appear in RePEc, Research Papers in Economics http://repec.org/ and are highly ranked in Google and Google Scholar.

Please enter the year this repository launched.

1995

Which subject area(s) does the repository serve?

Agricultural and applied economics

Which languages are included in the repository?

Any language

Which software does the repository use?

DSpace

Software was developed for the repository.

Which resources or tools does the repository offer?

Newsletter

Facebook

Twitter

AGECON SEARCH REPOSITORY ORIGINS

What were the motivating factors that led to the creation of a repository in this field/on this subject?

A desire to alleviate barriers to accessing literature or other resources within the discipline

Expressions of community readiness (quantitative, qualitative, or anecdotal evidence that a central resource is needed)

Which planning activities did you complete before launching this repository?

Stakeholder focus group

Environmental scanning

AGECON SEARCH REPOSITORY AUDIENCE

Who is the primary audience of this repository?

Academics

Government

Students

Do you have a sense of how large the repository's primary audience might be?

Yes

If yes, how did you determine the size of this audience?

Size of disciplinary research community

To the extent possible, please estimate what percentage of your primary audience contributes to the repository.

50%

AgEcon Search Repository Content

What strategies are used to recruit content for the repository?

Submissions are moderated by repository staff to make sure they are within the scope of the resource.

Submissions are arranged through formal arrangements with publishers.

Submissions are arranged through formal arrangements with professional organizations.

Submissions are arranged through formal arrangements with research centers.

Which content types are accepted in the repository?

Working papers

Pre-prints

Post-prints

Book chapters

Books

Datasets

Dissertations

Theses

Reports

Conference papers, journal articles, government documents

How many digital objects (e.g., full text items, datasets, etc.) does the repository contain? Digital objects are distinct from metadata records. An estimate is acceptable.

66,000

How do you promote use of or deposit in this repository to the community it serves?

Conference presentations

Email announcements

Newsletters

Partnerships with scholarly societies

Exhibits at conferences

Have recent government mandates affected the repository's collection development?

Not yet, but this is anticipated.

AgEcon Search Repository Metadata

Please indicate which metadata fields are required for deposition of content.

Title

Creator

Identifier

Date published

Language

Who enters descriptive metadata for repository content?

Authors

Student workers

How many metadata records does the repository contain? Metadata records are the total number of records, which include both records that represent digital objects held in the repository and records that link to materials outside of the repository. An estimate is acceptable.

66,000

Please indicate which descriptive tools are used in this repository.

Local or customized vocabularies

Uncontrolled vocabularies (i.e., user tags, author keywords)

AgEcon Search Organizational Structure and Staffing

Please indicate the organizational structure of the personnel in your library who administer the disciplinary repository.

A committee/group of staff from the library and other departments in the institution

Please enter the name of the library department/group that administers the repository, the number of individuals in the department/group, and the FTE (e.g., Individuals: 3, FTE: 3 or Individuals: 3, FTE: 2.5).

Department/group name: Research and Learning - Agriculture, Biology, Environment
Number of individuals: 8
Total FTE: 7.8

Please enter the position title for up to six individuals who administer the repository. Use official job titles when possible, or "intern," "volunteer," etc. If you are reporting on multiple positions that have varying levels of repository responsibility, please start with the position that has the most responsibility and work down.

Position 1   Science Librarian
Position 2   Library Assistant II
Position 3   Student

Please indicate whether each position is full-time permanent, part-time permanent, or temporary (e.g., grant-funded, internship, etc.)

Position 1   Part-time (permanent)
Position 2   Full-time (permanent)
Position 3   Temporary (part-time)

For each position, indicate the degree(s) that the individual holds.

Position 1   MLS/MLIS/PhD in Library and/or Information Science
             Masters in Biology
             Bachelor's or Associate degree
Position 2   Bachelor's or Associate degree
Position 3   NA

Please indicate whether each position has specialized subject knowledge related to the repository's discipline(s)/subject area(s).

Position 1   No
Position 2   No
Position 3   No

AGECON SEARCH REPOSITORY ADVISORY BOARD

Is there an external advisory board for this repository?

Yes

Please indicate which sectors the members of the advisory board represent.

Academics

Government

What level of influence does your advisory board have over the following areas? Please rate the level of influence on a scale of 1 to 4 where 1 is No influence and 4 is Large influence.

Strategic direction	Medium influence
Repository policies	Medium influence
Collection development activities	Small influence
Sustainability	Medium influence
Fundraising	Medium influence
Outreach	Medium influence
Day-to-day workflows	No influence

AgEcon Search Repository Funding

How is this disciplinary repository funded?

Internal library regular budget

One-time supplemental funds

Endowment fund

External grant funding

If your library received external grant funding, please identify the funding agency(ies).

USDA National Agriculture Library, CME Foundation, Farm Foundation, AAEA Trust

Does the current funding model appear to be sustainable?

Yes

Is there a sustainability plan for the repository?

No

What is the annual expense for the disciplinary repository (including personnel and equipment)? An estimate is acceptable.

$102,000

AgEcon Search Assessment

Has your library assessed the effectiveness of the repository?

Not yet, but we plan to.

If yes, or you plan to, please indicate the assessment method(s).

Collection and analysis of web usage statistics

Collection and analysis of download counts

User surveys

Interviews with individuals who use the repository

AgEcon Search Additional Comments

Please enter any additional information that may assist the authors' understanding of this disciplinary repository.

AgEcon Search began as a local solution for working papers produced and distributed by the University of Minnesota and 2 to 3 other mid-western universities. It is now an international resource, and functions as a distributed network. Users either upload their own papers (individual authors or one person on behalf of the organization) or reimburse our students to do it for them.

PubMed Central® (PMC) Repository Description

Please enter a brief description of the disciplinary repository.

PubMed Central® (PMC) is a free archive of biomedical and life sciences journal literature at the US National Institutes of Health's National Library of Medicine (NIH/NLM). In keeping with NLM's legislative mandate to collect and preserve the biomedical literature, PMC serves as a digital counterpart to NLM's extensive print journal collection. Launched in February 2000 it is managed by the National Center for Biotechnology Information (NCBI).

Please enter the year this repository launched.

2000

Which subject area(s) does the repository serve?

Biomedicine

Which languages are included in the repository?

English only

Which software does the repository use?

Software was developed for the repository.

Which resources or tools does the repository offer?

Publicly accessible website, http://www.ncbi.nlm.nih.gov/pmc/, offers a variety of resources.

PMC Repository Origins

What were the motivating factors that led to the creation of a repository in this field/on this subject?

A desire to alleviate barriers to accessing literature or other resources within the discipline

A call from the community to build a centralized resource

A call from a funder to build a centralized resource

Which planning activities did you complete before launching this repository?

NIH had a need to share the results of biomedical research with the biomedical community and the general public. This began as a voluntary process and later was mandated by the US Congress.

PMC Repository Audience

Who is the primary audience of this repository?

Academics

Industry

Government

Non-profit workers

General public

Students

Do you have a sense of how large the repository's primary audience might be?

No

To the extent possible, please estimate what percentage of your primary audience contributes to the repository.

None reported.

PMC REPOSITORY CONTENT

What strategies are used to recruit content for the repository?

Submissions are moderated by repository staff to make sure they are within the scope of the resource.

Submissions are arranged through formal arrangements with publishers.

Submissions are arranged through formal arrangements with funding bodies.

NIH, and certain other major research funding agencies, requires that peer-reviewed manuscripts supported by their funds be deposited in PMC.

Which content types are accepted in the repository?

Peer reviewed journal articles and author manuscripts, post peer review that have been accepted for publication by a journal.

How many digital objects (e.g., full text items, datasets, etc.) does the repository contain? Digital objects are distinct from metadata records. An estimate is acceptable.

2.8 million full-text articles

How do you promote use of or deposit in this repository to the community it serves?

Links to the repository from the PubMed citation database and other systems. NIH Public Access deposit requirement for grantees.

Have recent government mandates affected the repository's collection development?

Yes

If yes, please describe the impact.

A congressional mandate requires NIH funded manuscripts to be deposited, which has enriched the PMC database and increased its usage.

PMC REPOSITORY METADATA

Please indicate which metadata fields are required for deposition of content.

Title

Creator

Publisher

Date published

Language

Funding/grant data

Who enters descriptive metadata for repository content? Check all that apply.

Authors

See also http://www.ncbi.nlm.nih.gov/pmc/pub/pubinfo/

How many metadata records does the repository contain? Metadata records are the total number of records, which include both records that represent digital objects held in the repository and records that link to materials outside of the repository. An estimate is acceptable.

Over 2.8 million

Please indicate which descriptive tools are used in this repository.

Standardized vocabularies (i.e., LCSH, MeSH, NanoParticle Ontology)

If standardized vocabularies are used, please identify them.

MeSH

PMC Organizational Structure and Staffing

Please indicate which of the following best describes the organizational structure of the personnel in your library who administer the disciplinary repository.

A committee/group of staff from two or more departments within the library

Please enter the name of the library department/group that administers the repository, the number of individuals in the department/group, and the FTE (e.g., Individuals: 3, FTE: 3 or Individuals: 3, FTE: 2.5).

Department/group name: National Center for Biotechnology Information, Division of Library Operations

Please enter the position title for up to six individuals who administer the repository. Use official job titles when possible, or "intern," "volunteer," etc. If you are reporting on multiple positions that have varying levels of repository responsibility, please start with the position that has the most responsibility and work down.

Staffing for PMC is composed of positions ranging from computer scientists to librarians to content specialist. Level of degrees include BS, MS, and PhD.

PMC Repository Advisory Board

Is there an external advisory board for this repository?

Yes

Please indicate which sectors the members of the advisory board represent.

Academics

Industry

General public

Publishers. Current members of the advisory committee are listed at http://www.ncbi.nlm.nih.gov/pmc/about/nac/

What level of influence does your advisory board have over the following areas? Please rate the level of influence on a scale of 1 to 4 where 1 is No influence and 4 is Large influence.

Strategic direction	Large influence
Repository policies	Medium influence
Collection development activities	Medium influence
Sustainability	Small influence
Fundraising	No influence
Outreach	Medium influence
Day-to-day workflows	No influence

PMC Repository Funding

How is this disciplinary repository funded?

Parent institution budget

Does the current funding model appear to be sustainable?

Yes

Is there a sustainability plan for the repository?

Yes

What is the annual expense for the disciplinary repository (including personnel and equipment)? An estimate is acceptable.

None reported.

PMC Assessment

Has your library assessed the effectiveness of the repository?

Yes

If yes, or you plan to, please indicate the assessment method(s).

Collection and analysis of web usage statistics

Collection and analysis of download counts

PMC currently has 800K–950K users and 1.7M–1.8M full-text articles retrieved, per day.

HABRI Central Repository Description

Please enter a brief description of the disciplinary repository.

HABRI Central is an online platform for open research and collaboration into the relationships between humans and animals, specifically companion animals. HABRI Central uses a combination of library resources to facilitate the discovery, access, production, and preservation of human-animal interaction research. A bibliography of references to human-animal interaction literature helps you to discover existing research while a full-text repository allows you to freely access a wide-array of materials and tools. Along with these library resources, community-driven discussion areas, blogs, and user groups all allow you to connect and share knowledge with experts, professionals, and others involved in the study of human-animal interaction. By hosting all of these features in an easily accessible and centralized way, HABRI Central helps unite those involved in the study of human-animal interaction across disciplines while simultaneously lowering access barriers that might prevent the free flow of information among them.

Please enter the year this repository launched.

2012

Which subject area(s) does the repository serve?

The study of human-animal interaction

Which languages are included in the repository?

Any language

Which software does the repository use?

HUBzero http://www.hubzero.org

Which resources or tools does the repository offer?

Discussion forum

Newsletter

Calendar

Blog

Hosting of simulation tools and statistical packages

HABRI CENTRAL REPOSITORY ORIGINS

What were the motivating factors that led to the creation of a repository in this field/on this subject?

A desire to centralize distributed research

A desire to alleviate barriers to accessing literature or other resources within the discipline

A desire to increase visibility of the discipline's scholarship

Opportunity to leverage funding to build a resource that serves the discipline

Expressions of community readiness (quantitative, qualitative, or anecdotal evidence that a central resource is needed)

A call from the community to build a centralized resource

A call from a funder to build a centralized resource

Which planning activities did you complete before launching this repository?

Stakeholder workshop

Environmental scanning

Wrote strategic plan

Formed advisory board

Researched repository software

Researched repository features

Commissioned a sustainability plan and a market survey from consultants.

HABRI CENTRAL REPOSITORY AUDIENCE

Who is the primary audience of this repository?

Academics

Industry

Government

Non-profit workers

Animal-assisted therapists, animal welfare workers, and the other "expert amateurs" who use animals in health-related settings but do not usually get paid to do so.

Do you have a sense of how large the repository's primary audience might be?

Yes

If yes, how did you determine the size of this audience?

Size of disciplinary research community

Size of the industry market

To the extent possible, please estimate what percentage of your primary audience contributes to the repository.

<1%

Please enter any comments you may have on this repository's audience.

While we have plenty of evidence that the community uses the repository's resources they do not find the process of submitting content straightforward. This is substantially due to the fact that HUBzero was designed for academic users and is not user-friendly in the way it accepts submissions. We have been working with the developers on streamlining the submission process.

HABRI CENTRAL REPOSITORY CONTENT

What strategies are used to recruit content for the repository?

Anyone can create an account and submit materials.

Submissions are moderated by repository staff to make sure they are within the scope of the resource.

Submissions are arranged through formal arrangements with publishers.

The repository staff create content.

Authors are paid through the repository budget to create content.

We search other repositories and link to open access content that is hosted at a stable URL, adding keywords.

Which content types are accepted in the repository?

Abstracts

Working papers

Pre-prints

Post-prints

Book chapters

Books

Datasets

Slides

Video

Software components

References

Dissertations

Theses

Reports

Teaching objects

How many digital objects (e.g., full text items, datasets, etc.) does the repository contain? Digital objects are distinct from metadata records. An estimate is acceptable.

About 400

How do you promote use of or deposit in this repository to the community it serves?

Email announcements

Newsletters

Have recent government mandates affected the repository's collection development?

Not yet, but this is anticipated.

If yes or anticipated, please describe the impact.

This will hopefully makes a lot more relevant contact available through institutional, federal, or publisher repositories which we can then link to without having to clear rights ourselves.

HABRI CENTRAL REPOSITORY METADATA

Please indicate which metadata fields are required for deposition of content.

Title

Creator

Identifier

Publisher

Date published

Who enters descriptive metadata for repository content?

Authors

Repository staff

Student workers

Author entries are checked and enriched by repository staff.

How many metadata records does the repository contain? Metadata records are the total number of records, which include both records that represent digital objects held in the repository and records that link to materials outside of the repository. An estimate is acceptable.

17,000

Please indicate which descriptive tools are used in this repository.

Local or customized vocabularies

We are developing our own ontology since existing ones do not cover the field in a way that is useful for its community.

HABRI CENTRAL ORGANIZATIONAL STRUCTURE AND STAFFING

Please indicate the organizational structure of the personnel in your library who administer the disciplinary repository.

The project manager is employed entirely on grant funds and operates remotely. Two library faculty members provide portions of time. A repository specialist gives 75% effort. The Director of the University Press (UP), which is part of the University Libraries, also gives a small percentage of effort. There is a half-time graduate assistant and undergraduate student labor. It is a distributed enterprise. The strategic lead on the project is Charles Watkinson, Director of Purdue UP and Head of Scholarly Publishing Services in Purdue University Libraries.

Please enter the name of the library department/group that administers the repository, the number of individuals in the department/group, and the FTE (e.g., Individuals: 3, FTE: 3 or Individuals: 3, FTE: 2.5).

Department/group name: Libraries Publishing Division
Number of individuals: Not reported
Total FTE: 2.35

Please enter the position title for up to six individuals who administer the repository. Use official job titles when possible, or "intern," "volunteer," etc. If you are reporting on multiple positions that have varying levels of repository responsibility, please start with the position that has the most responsibility and work down.

Position 1	Project Manager
Position 2	Digital Repository Specialist
Position 3	Bibliographer
Position 4	Taxonomy Specialist
Position 5	Production Editor
Position 6	Graduate Assistant

Please indicate whether each position is full-time permanent, part-time permanent, or temporary (e.g., grant-funded, internship, etc.)

Position 1	Full-time (permanent)
Position 2	Part-time (permanent)
Position 3	Part-time (permanent)
Position 4	Part-time (permanent)
Position 5	Part-time (permanent)
Position 6	Temporary (part-time)

For each position, indicate the degree(s) that the individual holds. Check all that apply.

Position 1	Masters in a discipline other than library and information sciences
Position 2	MLS/MLIS/PhD in Library and/or Information Science
Position 3	MLS/MLIS/PhD in Library and/or Information Science
Position 4	MLS/MLIS/PhD in Library and/or Information Science
Position 5	Bachelor's or Associate degree
Position 6	Bachelor's or Associate degree

If you selected Masters or PhD in a discipline other than library and information sciences, please indicate the disciplines for the graduate degree.

Position 1	Communications

Please indicate whether each position has specialized subject knowledge related to the repository's discipline(s)/subject area(s).

Position 1	No
Position 2	No
Position 3	Yes: Veterinary librarian
Position 4	Yes: Health sciences librarian

Position 5   Yes: Background in medical publishing

Position 6   Yes: Graduate student in epidemiology

HABRI CENTRAL REPOSITORY ADVISORY BOARD

Is there an external advisory board for this repository?

Yes

Please indicate which sectors the members of the advisory board represent.

Academics

Industry

General public

Non-profit workers

There is a Management Advisory Board and an Editorial Board. The two are separate. I will answer on behalf of the Management Advisory Board for the following questions.

What level of influence does your advisory board have over the following areas? Please rate the level of influence on a scale of 1 to 4 where 1 is No influence and 4 is Large influence.

Strategic direction	Large influence
Repository policies	Large influence
Collection development activities	Small influence
Sustainability	Large influence
Fundraising	Small influence
Outreach	Large influence
Day-to-day workflows	Small influence

HABRI CENTRAL REPOSITORY FUNDING

How is this disciplinary repository funded?

External grant funding

If your library received external grant funding, please identify the funding agency(ies).

HABRI Foundation http://www.habri.org

Does the current funding model appear to be sustainable?

Yes

Yes in the short to medium term. In the longer term a model of commercial sponsorship from certain supporters of the HABRI Foundation, i.e., the pet care industry, looks feasible as this project is inexpensive in relation to the overall industry expenditures.

Is there a sustainability plan for the repository?

Yes

What is the annual expense for the disciplinary repository (including personnel and equipment)? An estimate is acceptable.

$350,000

HABRI CENTRAL ASSESSMENT

Has your library assessed the effectiveness of the repository?

Yes

If yes, or you plan to, please indicate the assessment method(s).

Collection and analysis of web usage statistics

Collection and analysis of download counts

Interviews with individuals who use the repository

Interviews with focus groups that use the repository

HABRI CENTRAL ADDITIONAL COMMENTS

Please enter any additional information that may assist the authors' understanding of this disciplinary repository.

Research into human-animal interaction is increasingly receiving respect in health circles, including several rounds of funding from NIH. HABRI Central is very much oriented toward translating research findings into practically implementable strategies.

INDUSTRY STUDIES WORKING PAPERS REPOSITORY DESCRIPTION

Please enter a brief description of the disciplinary repository.

The Industry Studies Working Paper Series brings together research from a wide range of academic disciplines. Papers published to the series reflect the knowledge of scholars who have made significant personal investments of time in learning about the market and firm institutions concerning the industries that they study.

Please enter the year this repository launched.

2010

Which subject area(s) does the repository serve?

Industry studies

Which languages are included in the repository?

English only

Which software does the repository use?

EPrints

Which resources or tools does the repository offer?

None reported.

INDUSTRY STUDIES WORKING PAPERS REPOSITORY ORIGINS

What were the motivating factors that led to the creation of a repository in this field/on this subject?

A desire to centralize distributed research

A desire to alleviate barriers to accessing literature or other resources within the discipline

A desire to increase visibility of the discipline's scholarship

A call from a professional society to build a centralized resource

Which planning activities did you complete before launching this repository?

Environmental scanning

Researched repository features

INDUSTRY STUDIES WORKING PAPERS REPOSITORY AUDIENCE

Who is the primary audience of this repository?

Academics

Industry

Government

Do you have a sense of how large the repository's primary audience might be?

No

To the extent possible, please estimate what percentage of your primary audience contributes to the repository.

None reported.

INDUSTRY STUDIES WORKING PAPERS REPOSITORY CONTENT

What strategies are used to recruit content for the repository?

Submissions are moderated by repository staff to make sure they are within the scope of the resource.

Submissions are peer reviewed by an editorial board affiliated with the repository.

The repository staff create content.

Which content types are accepted in the repository?

Working papers

How many digital objects (e.g., full text items, datasets, etc.) does the repository contain? Digital objects are distinct from metadata records. An estimate is acceptable.

130

How do you promote use of or deposit in this repository to the community it serves?

Email announcements

Have recent government mandates affected the repository's collection development?

No

INDUSTRY STUDIES WORKING PAPERS REPOSITORY METADATA

Please indicate which metadata fields are required for deposition of content.

Title

Creator

Date published

Date, format, status, refereed, et al.

Who enters descriptive metadata for repository content?

Authors

Repository staff

How many metadata records does the repository contain? Metadata records are the total number of records, which include both records that represent digital objects held in the repository and records that link to materials outside of the repository. An estimate is acceptable.

130

Please indicate which descriptive tools are used in this repository.

Uncontrolled vocabularies (i.e., user tags, author keywords)

INDUSTRY STUDIES WORKING PAPERS ORGANIZATIONAL STRUCTURE AND STAFFING

Please indicate the organizational structure of the personnel in your library who administer the disciplinary repository.

A single department in the library & faculty/staff in the Katz School of Business, University of Pittsburgh

Please enter the name of the library department/group that administers the repository, the number of individuals in the department/group, and the FTE (e.g., Individuals: 3, FTE: 3 or Individuals: 3, FTE: 2.5).

Department/group name:	Department of Information Technology, University Library System, and editor & staff of Industry Studies Working Papers/Industry Studies Association
Number of individuals:	6
Total FTE:	5

Please enter the position title for up to six individuals who administer the repository. Use official job titles when possible, or "intern," "volunteer," etc. If you are reporting on multiple positions that have varying levels of repository responsibility, please start with the position that has the most responsibility and work down.

Position 1	Director, Office of Scholarly Communication and Publishing
Position 2	Scholarly Communications Librarian
Position 3	Assistant Scholarly Communications Librarian
Position 4	Editor
Position 5	Student employee #1
Position 6	Student employee #2

Please indicate whether each position is full-time permanent, part-time permanent, or temporary (e.g., grant-funded, internship, etc.)

Position 1	Full-time (permanent)
Position 2	Full-time (permanent)
Position 3	Full-time (permanent)
Position 4	Full-time (permanent)
Position 5	Temporary (part-time)
Position 6	Temporary (part-time)

For each position, indicate the degree(s) that the individual holds. Check all that apply.

Position 1	MLS/MLIS/PhD in Library and/or Information Science
Position 2	MLS/MLIS/PhD in Library and/or Information Science
Position 3	MLS/MLIS/PhD in Library and/or Information Science
Position 4	PhD in a discipline other than library and information sciences
Position 5	MLS/MLIS/PhD in Library and/or Information Science
Position 6	MLS/MLIS/PhD in Library and/or Information Science

If you selected Masters or PhD in a discipline other than library and information sciences, please indicate the disciplines for the graduate degree.

Position 4	Business

Please indicate whether each position has specialized subject knowledge related to the repository's discipline(s)/subject area(s).

Position 1	No
Position 2	No
Position 3	No
Position 4	Yes: Subject knowledge of business/industry studies
Position 5	No
Position 6	Yes: Graduate student in business/industry studies

INDUSTRY STUDIES WORKING PAPERS REPOSITORY ADVISORY BOARD

Is there an external advisory board for this repository?

No

INDUSTRY STUDIES WORKING PAPERS REPOSITORY FUNDING

How is this disciplinary repository funded?

Internal library regular budget

Does the current funding model appear to be sustainable?

Yes

Is there a sustainability plan for the repository?

No

What is the annual expense for the disciplinary repository (including personnel and equipment)? An estimate is acceptable.

None reported.

INDUSTRY STUDIES WORKING PAPERS REPOSITORY ASSESSMENT

Has your library assessed the effectiveness of the repository?

No, and we have no plans to.

INTERNANO REPOSITORY DESCRIPTION

Please enter a brief description of the disciplinary repository.

InterNano, a service of the National Nanomanufacturing Network, informs and connects the nanomanufacturing community of researchers and practitioners. InterNano creates, collects, contextualizes, and disseminates relevant and timely resources, such as news highlights, reviews, processes, and topical assessments of the current state of practice in nanomanufacturing. Visitors can both use these resources and contribute information to the InterNano knowledgebase. InterNano works cooperatively with complementary informatics initiatives to facilitate data sharing among groups engaged with aspects of nanomanufacturing.

Please enter the year this repository launched.

2007

Which subject area(s) does the repository serve?

Nanomanufacturing

Which languages are included in the repository?

English only

Which software does the repository use?

EPrints

Joomla!, Drupal

Which resources or tools does the repository offer?

Email discussion list

Newsletter

Calendar

Directory

Facebook

Twitter

LinkedIn

Original articles, expert reviews, columns, and a nanomanufacturing process database

INTERNANO REPOSITORY ORIGINS

What were the motivating factors that led to the creation of a repository in this field/on this subject?

A desire to centralize distributed research

A desire to increase visibility of the discipline's scholarship

Part of a "broader impacts" strategy of a large research center.

Which planning activities did you complete before launching this repository?

Stakeholder charrette

Environmental scanning

User survey

Wrote strategic plan

Formed advisory board

Researched repository software

Researched repository features

InterNano Repository Audience

Who is the primary audience of this repository?

Academics

Industry

Government

Do you have a sense of how large the repository's primary audience might be?

Yes

If yes, how did you determine the size of this audience?

Size of disciplinary research community

Size of the industry market

Size of the government stakeholders

To the extent possible, please estimate what percentage of your primary audience contributes to the repository.

None specified.

Please enter any comments you may have on this repository's audience.

Audience size is very difficult to gauge because InterNano serves multiple disciplines and sectors. Also, users are one audience group and contributors are another. We have about 450 times the number of visitors/subscribers to our newsletter than we have people who contribute their work. We also aggregate existing research, press releases, and other content, which represents a much broader scope of authorship, but not active contributors.

InterNano Repository Content

What strategies are used to recruit content for the repository?

Anyone can create an account and submit materials.

Submissions are moderated by repository staff to make sure they are within the scope of the resource.

Submissions are arranged through formal arrangements with professional organizations.

The repository staff create content.

Authors are paid through the repository budget to create content.

Repository staff searches for relevant content and obtains permission to post it.

Which content types are accepted in the repository?

Abstracts

Working papers

Pre-prints

Post-prints

Book chapters

Books

Datasets

Slides

Video

Software components

References

Dissertations

Theses

Reports

Teaching objects

How many digital objects (e.g., full text items, datasets, etc.) does the repository contain? Digital objects are distinct from metadata records. An estimate is acceptable.

1003

How do you promote use of or deposit in this repository to the community it serves?

Advertising

Conference presentations

Newsletters

Have recent government mandates affected the repository's collection development?

No

InterNano Repository Metadata

Please indicate which metadata fields are required for deposition of content.

Title

Creator

Identifier

Publisher

Date published

Item type

Who enters descriptive metadata for repository content?

Authors

Repository staff

Student workers

How many metadata records does the repository contain? Metadata records are the total number of records, which include both records that represent digital objects held in the repository and records that link to materials outside of the repository. An estimate is acceptable.

1859

Please indicate which descriptive tools are used in this repository.

Local or customized vocabularies

Uncontrolled vocabularies (i.e., user tags, author keywords)

InterNano Organizational Structure and Staffing

Please indicate the organizational structure of the personnel in your library who administer the disciplinary repository.

A committee/group of staff from the library and other departments in the institution

Please enter the name of the library department/group that administers the repository, the number of individuals in the department/group, and the FTE (e.g., Individuals: 3, FTE: 3 or Individuals: 3, FTE: 2.5).

Department/group name:	Science and Engineering Library
Number of individuals:	4
Total FTE:	2

Please enter the position title for up to six individuals who administer the repository. Use official job titles when possible, or "intern," "volunteer," etc. If you are reporting on multiple positions that have varying levels of repository responsibility, please start with the position that has the most responsibility and work down.

Position 1	InterNano Project Manager/Science Librarian for the Center for Hierarchical Manufacturing
Position 2	Web/Database Developer
Position 3	National Nanomanufacturing Network Managing Director
Position 4	National Nanomanufacturing Network Director

Please indicate whether each position is full-time permanent, part-time permanent, or temporary (e.g., grant-funded, internship, etc.)

Position 1	Temporary (full-time)
Position 2	Temporary (part-time)
Position 3	Temporary (part-time)
Position 4	Part-time (permanent)

For each position, indicate the degree(s) that the individual holds.

Position 1	MLS/MLIS/PhD in Library and/or Information Science
Position 2	Bachelor's or Associate degree
Position 3	PhD in Electrical Engineering
Position 4	PhD in Physics

Please indicate whether each position has specialized subject knowledge related to the repository's discipline(s)/subject area(s).

Position 1	No
Position 2	No
Position 3	Yes: Electrical Engineering, nanomanufacturing
Position 4	Yes: Physics, nanomanufacturing

InterNano Repository Advisory Board

Is there an external advisory board for this repository?

Yes

Please indicate which sectors the members of the advisory board represent.

Academics

Industry

Government

What level of influence does your advisory board have over the following areas? Please rate the level of influence on a scale of 1 to 4 where 1 is No influence and 4 is Large influence.

Strategic direction	Large influence
Repository policies	Small influence
Collection development activities	Small influence
Sustainability	Large influence
Fundraising	No influence
Outreach	Small influence
Day-to-day workflows	No influence

InterNano Repository Funding

How is this disciplinary repository funded?

External grant funding

If your library received external grant funding, please identify the funding agency(ies).

National Science Foundation

Does the current funding model appear to be sustainable?

No

Comments: InterNano is funded through NSF grant CMMI-1025020, which expires in 2016. We are currently exploring alternate ways to fund InterNano.

Is there a sustainability plan for the repository?

No

What is the annual expense for the disciplinary repository (including personnel and equipment)? An estimate is acceptable.

$150,000 in direct costs

InterNano Assessment

Has your library assessed the effectiveness of the repository?

Yes

If yes, or you plan to, please indicate the assessment method(s).

Collection and analysis of web usage statistics

Collection and analysis of download counts

User surveys

Interviews with focus groups that use the repository

InterNano Additional Comments

Please enter any additional information that may assist the authors' understanding of this disciplinary repository.

The repository is a service of the National Nanomanufacturing Network (NNN), which is an alliance of academic, government, and industry partners that cooperate to advance nanomanufacturing strength in the US. The NNN is facilitated by a National Science Foundation Nanoscale Science and Engineering Center, the Center for Hierarchical Manufacturing. The NNN hosts workshops and conferences annually that InterNano staff help to plan. InterNano has "front end" site with value-added content, such as a directory, process database, taxonomy, and calendar. The NNN distributes a weekly newsletter that highlights InterNano content. InterNano and NNN staff are active members of a national nanoinformatics community.

The Aphasiology Archive Description

Please enter a brief description of the disciplinary repository.

The Aphasiology Archive is a repository of papers presented at the annual Clinical Aphasiology Conference (CAC). Papers provide information related to diagnosis, assessment, and treatment of persons with communication impairments—primarily those of aphasia but also including a restricted range of related disorders.

Please enter the year this repository launched.

2003

Which subject area(s) does the repository serve?

Communication impairments and disorders, Aphasia and aphasiology

Which languages are included in the repository?

English only

Which software does the repository use?

EPrints

Which resources or tools does the repository offer?

None reported.

THE APHASIOLOGY ARCHIVE ORIGINS

What were the motivating factors that led to the creation of a repository in this field/on this subject?

A desire to centralize distributed research

A desire to alleviate barriers to accessing literature or other resources within the discipline

A desire to increase visibility of the discipline's scholarship

A call from the community to build a centralized resource

Central location for papers and proposals presented at the annual Clinical Aphasiology Conference; online paper submission system provided by Department of Information Technology, University Library System, University of Pittsburgh.

Which planning activities did you complete before launching this repository?

Researched repository features

Discussion with stakeholders both at Pitt and externally, including Clinical Aphasiology Conference organizers.

THE APHASIOLOGY ARCHIVE AUDIENCE

Who is the primary audience of this repository?

Academics

Non-profit workers

Healthcare professionals

Do you have a sense of how large the repository's primary audience might be?

No

To the extent possible, please estimate what percentage of your primary audience contributes to the repository.

None reported.

THE APHASIOLOGY ARCHIVE CONTENT

What strategies are used to recruit content for the repository?

Submissions are peer reviewed by an editorial board affiliated with the repository.

Submissions are arranged through formal arrangements with professional organizations.

Submissions first are approved for presentation at the annual Clinical Aphasiology Conference, then harvested from the CAC conference papers site, http://cac.library.pitt.edu

Which content types are accepted in the repository?

Abstracts

Working papers

Citation-only records that link to published versions of papers presented

How many digital objects (e.g., full text items, datasets, etc.) does the repository contain? Digital objects are distinct from metadata records. An estimate is acceptable.

1450

How do you promote use of or deposit in this repository to the community it serves?

Conference presentations

Partnerships with scholarly societies

Have recent government mandates affected the repository's collection development?

No

Please indicate which metadata fields are required for deposition of content.

Title

Creator

Publisher

Date published

Conference title, location, and date

Who enters descriptive metadata for repository content?

Authors

Repository staff

Student workers

How many metadata records does the repository contain? Metadata records are the total number of records, which include both records that represent digital objects held in the repository and records that link to materials outside of the repository. An estimate is acceptable.

1734

Please indicate which descriptive tools are used in this repository.

Uncontrolled vocabularies (i.e., user tags, author keywords)

THE APHASIOLOGY ARCHIVE ORGANIZATIONAL STRUCTURE AND STAFFING

Please indicate the organizational structure of the personnel in your library who administer the disciplinary repository.

A single department within the library

Please enter the name of the library department/group that administers the repository, the number of individuals in the department/group, and the FTE (e.g., Individuals: 3, FTE: 3 or Individuals: 3, FTE: 2.5).

Department/group name:	Department of Information Technology
Number of individuals:	4
Total FTE:	3

Please enter the position title for up to six individuals who administer the repository. Use official job titles when possible, or "intern," "volunteer," etc. If you are reporting on multiple positions that have varying levels of repository responsibility, please start with the position that has the most responsibility and work down.

Position 1	Scholarly Communications Librarian
Position 2	Asst. Scholarly Communications Librarian
Position 3	Head, Department of Information Technology
Position 4	Intern/Student Worker

Please indicate whether each position is full-time permanent, part-time permanent, or temporary (e.g., grant-funded, internship, etc.)

Position 1	Full-time (permanent)
Position 2	Full-time (permanent)
Position 3	Full-time (permanent)
Position 4	Temporary (part-time)

For each position, indicate the degree(s) that the individual holds. Check all that apply.

Position 1	MLS/MLIS/PhD in Library and/or Information Science
Position 2	MLS/MLIS/PhD in Library and/or Information Science
Position 3	MLS/MLIS/PhD in Library and/or Information Science
Position 4	MLS/MLIS/PhD in Library and/or Information Science

Please indicate whether each position has specialized subject knowledge related to the repository's discipline(s)/subject area(s).

Position 1	No
Position 2	No
Position 3	No
Position 4	No

THE APHASIOLOGY ARCHIVE ADVISORY BOARD

Is there an external advisory board for this repository?

No

THE APHASIOLOGY ARCHIVE FUNDING

How is this disciplinary repository funded?

Internal library regular budget

Does the current funding model appear to be sustainable?

Yes

Is there a sustainability plan for the repository?

Yes

What is the annual expense for the disciplinary repository (including personnel and equipment)? An estimate is acceptable.

None reported.

THE APHASIOLOGY ARCHIVE ASSESSMENT

Has your library assessed the effectiveness of the repository?

No, and we have no plans to.

DRYAD REPOSITORY DESCRIPTION

Please enter a brief description of the disciplinary repository.

Dryad is a curated general-purpose repository that makes the data underlying scientific publications discoverable, freely reusable, and citable. Any journal or publisher that wishes to encourage data archiving may refer authors to Dryad. Dryad welcomes data submissions related to any published, or accepted, peer reviewed scientific and medical literature, particularly data for which no specialized repository exists.

Please enter the year this repository launched.

2008

Which subject area(s) does the repository serve?

Evolutionary Biology and Ecology

Which languages are included in the repository?

English only

Which software does the repository use?

DSpace

Software was developed for the repository

Which resources or tools does the repository offer?

Email discussion list

Blog

Facebook

Twitter

RSS Feeds, specialized APIs

DRYAD REPOSITORY ORIGINS

What were the motivating factors that led to the creation of a repository in this field/on this subject?

A desire to alleviate barriers to accessing literature or other resources within the discipline

Expressions of community readiness (quantitative, qualitative, or anecdotal evidence that a central resource is needed)

A call from the community to build a centralized resource

Need for preservation and archiving policies that cross disciplines.

Which planning activities did you complete before launching this repository?

Stakeholder workshop

Environmental scanning

Author survey

User survey

Formed advisory board

Researched repository software

Researched repository features

DRYAD REPOSITORY AUDIENCE

Who is the primary audience of this repository?

Academics

Students

Publishers, learned societies, institutions of research and education, funding bodies

Do you have a sense of how large the repository's primary audience might be?

No

Dryad Repository Content

What strategies are used to recruit content for the repository?

Anyone can create an account and submit materials.

Submissions are moderated by repository staff to make sure they are within the scope of the resource.

Submissions are arranged through formal arrangements with publishers.

Which content types are accepted in the repository?

Datasets

Video

Software components

Photographs

How many digital objects (e.g., full text items, datasets, etc.) does the repository contain? Digital objects are distinct from metadata records. An estimate is acceptable.

3,823 data packages

How do you promote use of or deposit in this repository to the community it serves?

Advertising

Conference presentations

Email announcements

Newsletters

Partnerships with scholarly societies

Brochures, bookmarks and magnets. T-shirts and other gifts and accessories from the Dryad Shop.

Have recent government mandates affected the repository's collection development?

Yes

DRYAD REPOSITORY METADATA

Please indicate which metadata fields are required for deposition of content.

Title

Creator

Identifier

Publisher

Date published

Follows Dublin Core guidelines, approximately 40 fields required.

Who enters descriptive metadata for repository content?

Authors

Repository staff

Student workers

Repository staff review and format, edit, add keywords, correct line breaks, etc.

How many metadata records does the repository contain? Metadata records are the total number of records, which include both records that represent digital objects held in the repository and records that link to materials outside of the repository. An estimate is acceptable.

11,077 data files

Please indicate which descriptive tools are used in this repository.

Standardized vocabularies (i.e., LCSH, MeSH, NanoParticle Ontology)

Local or customized vocabularies

Uncontrolled vocabularies (i.e., user tags, author keywords)

If standardized vocabularies are used, please identify them.

ITIS, HIVE, LCNAF, LCSH, MeSH, NBII, TGN, UBio

DRYAD ORGANIZATIONAL STRUCTURE AND STAFFING

Please indicate the organizational structure of the personnel in your library who administer the disciplinary repository.

A 12-member Board of Directors elected by members. Board oversees nonprofit tax-exempt 501(c)3 "Dryad."

Please enter the name of the library department/group that administers the repository, the number of individuals in the department/group, and the FTE (e.g., Individuals: 3, FTE: 3 or Individuals: 3, FTE: 2.5).

Department/group name:	Dryad Project Personnel
Number of individuals:	7
Total FTE:	Not reported

Please enter the position title for up to six individuals who administer the repository. Use official job titles when possible, or "intern," "volunteer," etc. If you are reporting on multiple positions that have varying levels of repository responsibility, please start with the position that has the most responsibility and work down.

Position 1	Software Engineer
Position 2	Senior Curator
Position 3	Repository Architect
Position 4	User Experience Designer
Position 5	Assistant Director of Informatics
Position 6	Communications Coordinator
Comments	The 7th position is a Project Manager.

NOTE: These are listed in random order and may not match the following two questions.

Please indicate whether each position is full-time permanent, part-time permanent, or temporary (e.g., grant-funded, internship, etc.)

Position 1	Full-time (permanent)
Position 2	Full-time (permanent)
Position 3	Full-time (permanent)
Position 4	Part-time (permanent)
Position 5	Part-time (permanent)
Position 6	Part-time (permanent)

For each position, indicate the degree(s) that the individual holds.

Position 1	Bachelor's or Associate degree Other credentials or licensing
Position 2	MLS/MLIS/PhD in Library and/or Information Science
Position 3	PhD in Computer Science and Cognitive Science
Position 4	Bachelor's or Associate degree
Position 5	Bachelor's or Associate degree
Position 6	MLS/MLIS/PhD in Library and/or Information Science

DRYAD REPOSITORY ADVISORY BOARD

Is there an external advisory board for this repository?

Yes

Please indicate which sectors the members of the advisory board represent.

Academics

Industry

Non-profit workers

What level of influence does your advisory board have over the following areas? Please rate the level of influence on a scale of 1 to 4 where 1 is No influence and 4 is Large influence.

Strategic direction	Large influence
Repository policies	Medium influence
Collection development activities	Medium influence
Sustainability	Large influence
Fundraising	Large influence
Outreach	Large influence
Day-to-day workflows	No influence

DRYAD REPOSITORY FUNDING

How is this disciplinary repository funded?

External grant funding

Membership fees, data publication charges, foundations, private donors

If your library received external grant funding, please identify the funding agency(ies).

National Science Foundation (NSF)

Does the current funding model appear to be sustainable?

Yes

Is there a sustainability plan for the repository?

Yes

What is the annual expense for the disciplinary repository (including personnel and equipment)?
An estimate is acceptable.

None reported.

DRYAD ASSESSMENT

Has your library assessed the effectiveness of the repository?

Yes

If yes, or you plan to, please indicate the assessment method(s).

Collection and analysis of web usage statistics

User surveys

Interviews with individuals who use the repository

Tracking backlinks

THE PHILSCI-ARCHIVE DESCRIPTION

Please enter a brief description of the disciplinary repository.

The PhilSci-Archive is an electronic archive for preprints in the philosophy of science. It is offered as a free service to the philosophy of science community. The goal of the archive is to promote communication in the field by the rapid dissemination of new work. PhilSci-Archive invites submissions in all areas of philosophy of science, including general philosophy of science, philosophy of particular sciences (physics, biology, chemistry, psychology, etc.), feminist philosophy of science, socially relevant philosophy of science, history and philosophy of science and history of the philosophy of science.

Please enter the year this repository launched.

2001

Which subject area(s) does the repository serve?

Philosophy of science, including general philosophy of science, philosophy of particular sciences (physics, biology, chemistry, psychology, etc.), feminist philosophy of science, socially relevant philosophy of science, history and philosophy of science and history of the philosophy of science.

Which languages are included in the repository?

English only

Which software does the repository use?

EPrints

Which resources or tools does the repository offer?

Email discussion list

Facebook

Twitter

RSS feeds, email sharing, other social media

The PhilSci-Archive Origins

What were the motivating factors that led to the creation of a repository in this field/on this subject?

A desire to centralize distributed research

A desire to alleviate barriers to accessing literature or other resources within the discipline

A desire to increase visibility of the discipline's scholarship

A call from the community to build a centralized resource

Which planning activities did you complete before launching this repository?

Formed advisory board

The PhilSci-Archive Audience

Who is the primary audience of this repository?

Academics

Do you have a sense of how large the repository's primary audience might be?

No

To the extent possible, please estimate what percentage of your primary audience contributes to the repository.

None reported.

The PhilSci-Archive Content

What strategies are used to recruit content for the repository?

Anyone can create an account and submit materials.

Submissions are moderated by repository staff to make sure they are within the scope of the resource.

Submissions are arranged through formal arrangements with professional organizations.

Which content types are accepted in the repository?

Pre-prints

How many digital objects (e.g., full text items, datasets, etc.) does the repository contain? Digital objects are distinct from metadata records. An estimate is acceptable.

3392

How do you promote use of or deposit in this repository to the community it serves?

Conference presentations

Email announcements

Partnerships with scholarly societies

Have recent government mandates affected the repository's collection development?

No

The PhilSci-Archive Metadata

Please indicate which metadata fields are required for deposition of content.

Title

Creator

Date published

Who enters descriptive metadata for repository content?

Authors

Repository staff

Student workers

How many metadata records does the repository contain? Metadata records are the total number of records, which include both records that represent digital objects held in the repository and records that link to materials outside of the repository. An estimate is acceptable.

None reported.

Please indicate which descriptive tools are used in this repository.

Uncontrolled vocabularies (i.e., user tags, author keywords)

THE PHILSCI-ARCHIVE ORGANIZATIONAL STRUCTURE AND STAFFING

Please indicate the organizational structure of the personnel in your library who administer the disciplinary repository.

A single department within the library

Please enter the name of the library department/group that administers the repository, the number of individuals in the department/group, and the FTE (e.g., Individuals: 3, FTE: 3 or Individuals: 3, FTE: 2.5).

Department/group name: None specified
Number of individuals: Not reported
Total FTE: 3.25

Please enter the position title for up to six individuals who administer the repository. Use official job titles when possible, or "intern," "volunteer," etc. If you are reporting on multiple positions that have varying levels of repository responsibility, please start with the position that has the most responsibility and work down.

Position 1   None specified
Position 2   None specified
Position 3   None specified
Position 4   None specified

Please indicate whether each position is full-time permanent, part-time permanent, or temporary (e.g., grant-funded, internship, etc.)

Position 1   Full-time (permanent)
Position 2   Full-time (permanent)
Position 3   Full-time (permanent)
Position 4   Temporary (part-time)

For each position, indicate the degree(s) that the individual holds. Check all that apply.

Position 1	MLS/MLIS/PhD in Library and/or Information Science
Position 2	MLS/MLIS/PhD in Library and/or Information Science
Position 3	MLS/MLIS/PhD in Library and/or Information Science
Position 4	MLS/MLIS/PhD in Library and/or Information Science

Please indicate whether each position has specialized subject knowledge related to the repository's discipline(s)/subject area(s).

Position 1	No
Position 2	No
Position 3	No
Position 4	No

THE PHILSCI-ARCHIVE ADVISORY BOARD

Is there an external advisory board for this repository?

Yes

Please indicate which sectors the members of the advisory board represent. Check all that apply.

Academics

THE PHILSCI-ARCHIVE FUNDING

How is this disciplinary repository funded?

Internal library regular budget

Does the current funding model appear to be sustainable?

Yes

Is there a sustainability plan for the repository?

Yes

What is the annual expense for the disciplinary repository (including personnel and equipment)? An estimate is acceptable.

None reported.

The PhilSci-Archive Assessment

Has your library assessed the effectiveness of the repository?

No, and we have no plans to.

Resources in Integrated Care for Morbidity Management and Disability Prevention Repository Description

Please enter a brief description of the disciplinary repository.

RIIC-4MMDP is a free, open access, online, self-archiving repository dedicated to sharing best practices, lessons learned, and exploring new strategies for morbidity management and disability prevention (MMDP) with the wider MMDP community. The primary goal is to aid countries as they build capacity for planning, implementing, monitoring and evaluating MMDP activities.

Please enter the year this repository launched.

2013

Which subject area(s) does the repository serve?

Neglected tropical diseases, disability prevention, early detection of disease and prevention

Which languages are included in the repository?

Any language

Which software does the repository use?

EPrints

Which resources or tools does the repository offer?

Email discussion list

RIIC-4MMDP Repository Origins

What were the motivating factors that led to the creation of a repository in this field/on this subject?

A desire to centralize distributed research

A desire to alleviate barriers to accessing literature or other resources within the discipline

A desire to increase visibility of the discipline's scholarship

Expressions of community readiness (quantitative, qualitative, or anecdotal evidence that a central resource is needed)

A call from a professional society to build a centralized resource

Which planning activities did you complete before launching this repository?

Stakeholder focus group

Wrote strategic plan

Formed advisory board

RIIC-4MMDP REPOSITORY AUDIENCE

Who is the primary audience of this repository?

Academics

Government

Non-profit workers

Medical care workers, field workers

Do you have a sense of how large the repository's primary audience might be?

No

To the extent possible, please estimate what percentage of your primary audience contributes to the repository.

None reported.

RIIC-4MMDP REPOSITORY CONTENT

What strategies are used to recruit content for the repository?

Anyone can create an account and submit materials.

Submissions are moderated by repository staff to make sure they are within the scope of the resource.

Submissions are arranged through formal arrangements with professional organizations.

Submissions are arranged through formal arrangements with research centers.

Submissions are arranged through formal arrangements with funding bodies.

The repository staff create content.

Which content types are accepted in the repository?

Working papers

Pre-prints

Post-prints

Book chapters

Books

Datasets

Slides

Video

Reports

Teaching objects

How many digital objects (e.g., full text items, datasets, etc.) does the repository contain? Digital objects are distinct from metadata records. An estimate is acceptable.

38 (the repository is under development at this writing)

How do you promote use of or deposit in this repository to the community it serves?

Conference presentations

Email announcements

Newsletters

Partnerships with non-profit entities involved in morbidity management and disease prevention.

Have recent government mandates affected the repository's collection development?

No

RIIC-4MMDP Repository Metadata

Please indicate which metadata fields are required for deposition of content.

Title

Creator

Identifier

Publisher

Date published

Language

Who enters descriptive metadata for repository content?

Authors

Repository staff

Student workers

How many metadata records does the repository contain? Metadata records are the total number of records, which include both records that represent digital objects held in the repository and records that link to materials outside of the repository. An estimate is acceptable.

38

Please indicate which descriptive tools are used in this repository.

Local or customized vocabularies

RIIC-4MMDP Organizational Structure and Staffing

Please indicate the organizational structure of the personnel in your library who administer the disciplinary repository.

A single library department, plus an editorial board of subject experts, plus an editor affiliated with the partner institution.

Please enter the name of the library department/group that administers the repository, the number of individuals in the department/group, and the FTE (e.g., Individuals: 3, FTE: 3 or Individuals: 3, FTE: 2.5).

Department/group name:	Office of Scholarly Communication and Publishing, University Library System, University of Pittsburgh
Number of individuals:	6
Total FTE:	5

Please enter the position title for up to six individuals who administer the repository. Use official job titles when possible, or "intern," "volunteer," etc. If you are reporting on multiple positions that have varying levels of repository responsibility, please start with the position that has the most responsibility and work down.

Position 1 Director, Office of Scholarly Communication and Publishing

Position 2 Scholarly Communications Librarian

Position 3 Assistant Scholarly Communications Librarian

Position 4 Solutions Architect

Position 5 Database Administrator

Position 6 Student employee

Please indicate whether each position is full-time permanent, part-time permanent, or temporary (e.g., grant-funded, internship, etc.)

Position 1 Full-time (permanent)

Position 2 Full-time (permanent)

Position 3 Full-time (permanent)

Position 4 Full-time (permanent)

Position 5 Full-time (permanent)

Position 6 Temporary (part-time)

For each position, indicate the degree(s) that the individual holds. Check all that apply.

Position 1 MLS/MLIS/PhD in Library and/or Information Science

Position 2 MLS/MLIS/PhD in Library and/or Information Science

Position 3 MLS/MLIS/PhD in Library and/or Information Science

Position 4 Bachelor's or Associate degree

Position 5 Bachelor's or Associate degree

Position 6 MLS/MLIS/PhD in Library and/or Information Science

Please indicate whether each position has specialized subject knowledge related to the repository's discipline(s)/subject area(s).

Position 1 No

Position 2 No

Position 3 No

Position 4 No

Position 5 No

Position 6 No

RIIC-4MMDP Repository Advisory Board

Is there an external advisory board for this repository?

Yes

Please indicate which sectors the members of the advisory board represent. Check all that apply.

Academics

Government

Non-profit workers

What level of influence does your advisory board have over the following areas? Please rate the level of influence on a scale of 1 to 4 where 1 is No influence and 4 is Large influence.

Strategic direction	Large influence
Repository policies	Medium influence
Collection development activities	Large influence
Sustainability	Large influence
Fundraising	Large influence
Outreach	Large influence
Day-to-day workflows	Small influence

RIIC-4MMDP Repository Funding

How is this disciplinary repository funded?

Internal library regular budget

External funding by non-profit partnership

Does the current funding model appear to be sustainable?

Yes

Is there a sustainability plan for the repository?

No

What is the annual expense for the disciplinary repository (including personnel and equipment)? An estimate is acceptable.

None reported.

RIIC-4MMDP Repository Assessment

Has your library assessed the effectiveness of the repository?

No, and we have no plans to.

The Archive of European Integration Repository Description

Please enter a brief description of the disciplinary repository.

The Archive of European Integration (AEI) was initiated and created by Dr. Phil Wilkin, Social Sciences Bibliographer, University Library System, University of Pittsburgh, AEI Editor, and Dr. Michael Nentwich, Austrian Academy of Sciences, Institute of Technology Assessment, Vienna, Austria. Nentwich is a managing editor of the European Research Papers Archive, the only other online repository dedicated to the collection of full text materials on European integration. Since the creation of the AEI in February 2003, the University Library System (ULS) has provided the technical and material support for the AEI. The task of designing and implementing the archive was undertaken by a team from the ULS Department of Information Systems including Timothy Deliyannides, Brian Gregg, Jeffrey Wisniewski and Demetrios Ioannides. The AEI is also supported by the European Union Center of Excellence and European Studies Center, University of Pittsburgh, and the European Union Studies Association (EUSA), housed at the University of Pittsburgh. Dr. Alberta Sbragia, former Director, European Union Center of Excellence and Center for European Studies, University of Pittsburgh, and current Vice Provost for Graduate Studies, University of Pittsburgh, serves as a consultant for AEI. Phil Wilkin administers all academic and intellectual aspects of the AEI. Since Fall 2004, Barbara Sloan, formerly Head of Public Inquiries, Delegation of the European Commission to the US, Washington, DC, has been active in all phases of the development of the AEI-EU section of the AEI.

Please enter the year this repository launched.

2002

Which subject area(s) does the repository serve?

European integration

Which languages are included in the repository?

Any language

Which software does the repository use?

EPrints

Which resources or tools does the repository offer?

Facebook

Twitter

The AEI Repository Origins

What were the motivating factors that led to the creation of a repository in this field/on this subject?

A desire to centralize distributed research A desire to alleviate barriers to accessing literature or other resources within the discipline

A desire to increase visibility of the discipline's scholarship

A call from the community to build a centralized resource

Which planning activities did you complete before launching this repository?

None reported.

The AEI Repository Audience

Who is the primary audience of this repository?

Academics

Non-profit workers

General public

Do you have a sense of how large the repository's primary audience might be?

No

To the extent possible, please estimate what percentage of your primary audience contributes to the repository.

None reported.

The AEI Repository Content

What strategies are used to recruit content for the repository?

Submissions are moderated by repository staff to make sure they are within the scope of the resource.

Submissions are arranged through formal arrangements with research centers.

The repository staff create content.

Which content types are accepted in the repository?

None reported.

How many digital objects (e.g., full text items, datasets, etc.) does the repository contain? Digital objects are distinct from metadata records. An estimate is acceptable.

27,171

How do you promote use of or deposit in this repository to the community it serves?

Conference presentations

Email announcements

Scholarly publications

Have recent government mandates affected the repository's collection development?

No

The AEI Repository Metadata

Please indicate which metadata fields are required for deposition of content.

Title

Creator

Date published

Who enters descriptive metadata for repository content?

Authors

Repository staff

Student workers

How many metadata records does the repository contain? Metadata records are the total number of records, which include both records that represent digital objects held in the repository and records that link to materials outside of the repository. An estimate is acceptable.

None reported.

Please indicate which descriptive tools are used in this repository.

Local or customized vocabularies

Uncontrolled vocabularies (i.e., user tags, author keywords)

Please indicate the organizational structure of the personnel in your library who administer the disciplinary repository.

A single department within the library

Please enter the name of the library department/group that administers the repository, the number of individuals in the department/group, and the FTE (e.g., Individuals: 3, FTE: 3 or Individuals: 3, FTE: 2.5).

Department/group name: None reported
Number of individuals: None reported
Total FTE: 3.5

Please enter the position title for up to six individuals who administer the repository. Use official job titles when possible, or "intern," "volunteer," etc. If you are reporting on multiple positions that have varying levels of repository responsibility, please start with the position that has the most responsibility and work down.

Position 1   None reported
Position 2   None reported
Position 3   None reported
Position 4   None reported

Please indicate whether each position is full-time permanent, part-time permanent, or temporary (e.g., grant-funded, internship, etc.)

Position 1   Full-time (permanent)
Position 2   Full-time (permanent)
Position 3   Full-time (permanent)
Position 4   Temporary (part-time)

For each position, indicate the degree(s) that the individual holds. Check all that apply.

Position 1   MLS/MLIS/PhD in Library and/or Information Science
Position 2   MLS/MLIS/PhD in Library and/or Information Science
Position 3   MLS/MLIS/PhD in Library and/or Information Science
Position 4   MLS/MLIS/PhD in Library and/or Information Science

Please indicate whether each position has specialized subject knowledge related to the repository's discipline(s)/subject area(s).

Position 1   None reported
Position 2   None reported
Position 3   None reported
Position 4   None reported

THE AEI REPOSITORY ADVISORY BOARD

Is there an external advisory board for this repository?

No

THE AEI REPOSITORY FUNDING

How is this disciplinary repository funded?

Internal library regular budget

Does the current funding model appear to be sustainable?

Yes

Is there a sustainability plan for the repository?

Yes

What is the annual expense for the disciplinary repository (including personnel and equipment)? An estimate is acceptable.

None reported.

THE AEI REPOSITORY ASSESSMENT

Has your library assessed the effectiveness of the repository?

No, and we have no plans to.

Please enter a brief description of the disciplinary repository.

The Digital Archaeological Record (tDAR) is an international digital repository for archaeological and related data. The repository contains data, documents, and other files related to a wide range of archaeological investigations and topics, e.g., archives and collections, field studies of various scales and intensities, and historical, methodological, synthetic, or theoretical studies. Repository administration, development, and maintenance are governed by the Center for Digital Antiquity, an organization dedicated to ensuring the long-term preservation of irreplaceable archaeological data and to broadening the access to these data.

Please enter the year this repository launched.

2009

Which subject area(s) does the repository serve?

Archaeology and related fields

Which languages are included in the repository?

Any language

Which software does the repository use?

Software was developed for the repository

Which resources or tools does the repository offer?

Newsletter

Blog

Facebook

Twitter

TDAR REPOSITORY ORIGINS

What were the motivating factors that led to the creation of a repository in this field/on this subject?

A desire to centralize distributed research

A desire to alleviate barriers to accessing literature or other resources within the discipline

A desire to increase visibility of the discipline's scholarship

Opportunity to leverage funding to build a resource that serves the discipline

Expressions of community readiness (quantitative, qualitative, or anecdotal evidence that a central resource is needed)

A call from the community to build a centralized resource

A call from a funder to build a centralized resource

Which planning activities did you complete before launching this repository?

Stakeholder workshop

Stakeholder focus group

Wrote strategic plan

Formed advisory board

Researched repository software

Researched repository features

Articles in professional journals and presentations at professional conferences and workshops

TDAR REPOSITORY AUDIENCE

Who is the primary audience of this repository?

Academics

Industry

Government

Students

The repository contents are not explicitly designed to be of interest to the general public, however, many of the visitors to the repository website appear to be members of the general public who have an interest in the archaeology of specific geographical areas or topics. We are pleased that the repository also is of interest to this audience and may in the future develop features that are of interest and relevance to such visitors and users.

Do you have a sense of how large the repository's primary audience might be?

Yes

If yes, how did you determine the size of this audience?

Size of disciplinary research community

Size of the industry market

Size of the government stakeholders

To the extent possible, please estimate what percentage of your primary audience contributes to the repository.

2%

Please enter any comments you may have on this repository's audience.

In a 2010 article Altschul and Patterson estimate the number of professional archaeologists in the US at about 9,000 in the academic, government, and consulting firm sectors. As of 1 September 2013, we have 215 individuals or organizations that have contributed files to tDAR. 215/9000 = 2.3%. We anticipate that the percentage of contributors from our primary audience will increase substantially over time.

tDAR Repository Content

What strategies are used to recruit content for the repository?

Anyone can create an account and submit materials.

Submissions are moderated by repository staff to make sure they are within the scope of the resource.

Submissions are arranged through formal arrangements with publishers.

Submissions are arranged through formal arrangements with professional organizations.

Submissions are arranged through formal arrangements with funding bodies.

The repository staff create content.

In 2011 and 2012, as part of our strategy to build tDAR content, create a user community, and test aspects of the repository software, the Center for Digital Antiquity provide small grants (ranging from $1,000 to $10,000/grant) to individuals and organizations to add content to tDAR. Approximately 25 grants totaling approximately $111,000 were distributed.

Which content types are accepted in the repository?

Working papers

Pre-prints

Post-prints

Book chapters

Books

Datasets

Slides

Dissertations

Theses

Reports

Teaching objects

Digital files of images (photos, maps, drawings, etc.); digital files of field and other research forms or notes; 3D scans of artifacts and archaeological landscapes.

How many digital objects (e.g., full text items, datasets, etc.) does the repository contain? Digital objects are distinct from metadata records. An estimate is acceptable.

As of 1 September 2013, tDAR contains: 552 data sets; 6,551 full text documents; 141 3D scans of artifacts; 16,919 images; and citation-only records for 357,068 documents.

How do you promote use of or deposit in this repository to the community it serves?

Advertising

Conference presentations

Email announcements

Newsletters

Partnerships with scholarly societies

Scholarly publications

Trade publications

Have recent government mandates affected the repository's collection development?

Yes

If yes, please describe the impact.

In both positive and negative ways recent government actions, including mandates have affected tDAR's content development. On the negative site, the budget cuts required by federal government sequestration have slowed the rate at which federal agency offices have decided to use tDAR to manage the archaeological information for which they are responsible. On the positive side, the Administration's developing policy of "Open Gov" and improving access to federal scientific data, including archaeological data, has created an interest in considering by federal agency offices in using tDAR to provide for this required access.

tDAR Repository Metadata

Please indicate which metadata fields are required for deposition of content.

Title

Creator

Publisher

Date published

Language

There are a number of additional metadata fields. See https://dev.tdar.org/confluence/display/TDAR/Data+Dictionary.

Who enters descriptive metadata for repository content?

Authors

Repository staff

Student workers

Third party

Via the tDAR website, metadata records can be created and files uploaded by any of these individuals. See http://www.
tdar.org/why-tdar/contribute/

How many metadata records does the repository contain? Metadata records are the total number of records, which include both records that represent digital objects held in the repository and records that link to materials outside of the repository. An estimate is acceptable.

390,000 metadata records

Please indicate which descriptive tools are used in this repository.

Local or customized vocabularies

Uncontrolled vocabularies (i.e., user tags, author keywords)

tDAR Organizational Structure and Staffing

Please indicate the organizational structure of the personnel in your library who administer the disciplinary repository.

The Center for Digital Antiquity has a staff of five full-time staff and four or five part-time staff. The Center is administered and staff are part of the School of Human Evolution and Social (SHESC) at ASU and housed in Hayden Library and work closely with ASU Libraries staff on a variety of projects and programs.

Please enter the name of the library department/group that administers the repository, the number of individuals in the department/group, and the FTE (e.g., Individuals: 3, FTE: 3 or Individuals: 3, FTE: 2.5).

Department/group name: The Center for Digital Antiquity
Number of individuals: 10
Total FTE: 6.6

Please enter the position title for up to six individuals who administer the repository. Use official job titles when possible, or "intern," "volunteer," etc. If you are reporting on multiple positions that have varying levels of repository responsibility, please start with the position that has the most responsibility and work down.

Position 1	Executive Director
Position 2	Director of Technology
Position 3	Programmer
Position 4	Marketing and Sales Coordinator
Position 5	Assistant to the Executive Director (part-time)
Position 6	Digital Curators (5)

Please indicate whether each position is full-time permanent, part-time permanent, or temporary (e.g., grant-funded, internship, etc.)

Position 1	Full-time (permanent)
Position 2	Full-time (permanent)
Position 3	Full-time (permanent)
Position 4	Full-time (permanent)
Position 5	Part-time (permanent)
Position 6	one Full-time (permanent); four Temporary (part time)

For each position, indicate the degree(s) that the individual holds.

Position 1	PhD in Anthropology/Archaeology
Position 2	Bachelor's or Associate degree
Position 3	Bachelor's or Associate degree
	Other credentials or licensing: Various software competency certificates
Position 4	Masters in Anthropology/Archaeology
Position 5	Bachelor's or Associate degree
Position 6	Masters in Anthropology/Archaeology

Please indicate whether each position has specialized subject knowledge related to the repository's discipline(s)/subject area(s).

Position 1	Yes: archaeology
Position 2	Yes: digital libraries, archaeology
Position 3	No
Position 4	Yes: archaeology
Position 5	No
Position 6	Yes: archaeology

TDAR REPOSITORY ADVISORY BOARD

Is there an external advisory board for this repository?

Yes

Please indicate which sectors the members of the advisory board represent.

Academics

Industry

Government

Non-profit workers

Business, Finance, Law

What level of influence does your advisory board have over the following areas? Please rate the level of influence on a scale of 1 to 4 where 1 is No influence and 4 is Large influence.

Strategic direction	Large influence
Repository policies	Large influence
Collection development activities	Large influence
Sustainability	Large influence
Fundraising	Medium influence
Outreach	Medium influence
Day-to-day workflows	Small influence

Comments: The Center has a Board of Directors, which is involved with policies, strategic direction, executive director evaluation, repository oversight, and general governance. The Center also has a Professional Advisory Panel, which advises on professional and technical development topics.

TDAR REPOSITORY FUNDING

How is this disciplinary repository funded?

External grant funding

Contracts for digital archiving services and digital curation services

If your library received external grant funding, please identify the funding agency(ies).

The Center has received external grant funding from the Andrew W. Mellon Foundation; National Science Foundation; National Endowment for the Humanities. Contracts from government agency offices, research organizations and projects, industry firms, and individual researchers.

Does the current funding model appear to be sustainable?

Yes

Is there a sustainability plan for the repository?

Yes

What is the annual expense for the disciplinary repository (including personnel and equipment)? An estimate is acceptable.

$800,000

tDAR Assessment

Has your library assessed the effectiveness of the repository?

Not yet, but we plan to

If yes, or you plan to, please indicate the assessment method(s).

Collection and analysis of web usage statistics

Collection and analysis of download counts

User surveys

Interviews with individuals who use the repository

Interviews with focus groups that use the repository

We may adopt other methods as well.

Minority Health and Health Equity Archive Description

Please enter a brief description of the disciplinary repository.

The Minority Health and Health Equity Archive focuses on providing access to materials in the fields of minority health and health disparities research and policy. The goal of the Archive is to promote trans-disciplinary scholarship on race, ethnicity and disparities research designed to achieve health equity.

Please enter the year this repository launched.

2004

Which subject area(s) does the repository serve?

Minority health, health disparities, ethnic and racial disparities in health research, policy, and services

Which languages are included in the repository?

English only

Which software does the repository use?

EPrints

Which resources or tools does the repository offer?

Facebook

Twitter

RSS feeds, other social media sharing

MHHE Archive Origins

What were the motivating factors that led to the creation of a repository in this field/on this subject?

A desire to centralize distributed research

A desire to alleviate barriers to accessing literature or other resources within the discipline

A desire to increase visibility of the discipline's scholarship

Which planning activities did you complete before launching this repository?

Formed advisory board

MHHE Archive Audience

Who is the primary audience of this repository?

Academics

Government

Non-profit workers

Do you have a sense of how large the repository's primary audience might be?

No

To the extent possible, please estimate what percentage of your primary audience contributes to the repository.

None reported.

What strategies are used to recruit content for the repository?

Anyone can create an account and submit materials.

Submissions are moderated by repository staff to make sure they are within the scope of the resource.

Submissions are arranged through formal arrangements with research centers.

Submissions are arranged through formal arrangements with funding bodies.

The repository staff create content.

Which content types are accepted in the repository?

Abstracts

Working papers

Post-prints

Book chapters

Slides

Video

Dissertations

Theses

Reports

Citation-only records

How many digital objects (e.g., full text items, datasets, etc.) does the repository contain? Digital objects are distinct from metadata records. An estimate is acceptable.

1000

How do you promote use of or deposit in this repository to the community it serves?

Conference presentations

Email announcements

Newsletters

Have recent government mandates affected the repository's collection development?

No

Please indicate which metadata fields are required for deposition of content.

Title

Creator

Publisher

Date published

Who enters descriptive metadata for repository content?

Authors

Repository staff

Student workers

How many metadata records does the repository contain? Metadata records are the total number of records, which include both records that represent digital objects held in the repository and records that link to materials outside of the repository. An estimate is acceptable.

2550

Please indicate which descriptive tools are used in this repository.

Local or customized vocabularies

Uncontrolled vocabularies (i.e., user tags, author keywords)

MHHE Archive Organizational Structure and Staffing

Please indicate the organizational structure of the personnel in your library who administer the disciplinary repository.

Repository is administered by library staff. Content is provided and editorial management is done by faculty and students at the Center for Health Equity, University of Maryland.

Please enter the name of the library department/group that administers the repository, the number of individuals in the department/group, and the FTE (e.g., Individuals: 3, FTE: 3 or Individuals: 3, FTE: 2.5).

Department/group name: Department of Information Technology, University Library System, University of Pittsburgh
Number of individuals: 3
Total FTE: 3

Please enter the position title for up to six individuals who administer the repository. Use official job titles when possible, or "intern," "volunteer," etc. If you are reporting on multiple positions that have varying levels of repository responsibility, please start with the position that has the most responsibility and work down.

Position 1   Director, Office of Scholarly Communication and Publishing

Position 2   Scholarly Communications Librarian

Position 3   Asst. Scholarly Communications Librarian

Comment: Other administrative staff assist on an as-needed basis with technology; the actual work of inputting records into the repository is done by University of Maryland staff.

Please indicate whether each position is full-time permanent, part-time permanent, or temporary (e.g., grant-funded, internship, etc.)

Position 1   Full-time (permanent)

Position 2   Full-time (permanent)

Position 3   Full-time (permanent)

For each position, indicate the degree(s) that the individual holds. Check all that apply.

Position 1   MLS/MLIS/PhD in Library and/or Information Science

Position 2   MLS/MLIS/PhD in Library and/or Information Science

Position 3   MLS/MLIS/PhD in Library and/or Information Science

Please indicate whether each position has specialized subject knowledge related to the repository's discipline(s)/subject area(s).

Position 1   No

Position 2   No

Position 3   No

MHHE Archive Advisory Board

Is there an external advisory board for this repository?

Yes

Please indicate which sectors the members of the advisory board represent.

Academics

What level of influence does your advisory board have over the following areas? Please rate the level of influence on a scale of 1 to 4 where 1 is No influence and 4 is Large influence.

Strategic direction	Large influence
Repository policies	Medium influence
Collection development activities	Large influence
Sustainability	Medium influence
Fundraising	Large influence
Outreach	Large influence
Day-to-day workflows	Large influence

MHHE ARCHIVE FUNDING

How is this disciplinary repository funded?

Internal library regular budget

External grant funding

Funding from the University of Maryland, separate from the University Library System, University of Pittsburgh, funding.

Does the current funding model appear to be sustainable?

Yes

Is there a sustainability plan for the repository?

No

What is the annual expense for the disciplinary repository (including personnel and equipment)? An estimate is acceptable.

None reported.

MHHE ARCHIVE ASSESSMENT

Has your library assessed the effectiveness of the repository?

No, and we have no plans to.

RESPONDING INSTITUTIONS

University at Albany, SUNY

University of Alberta

Arizona State University

Auburn University

University of Calgary

University of California, Irvine

Case Western Reserve University

University of Chicago

University of Colorado at Boulder

University of Connecticut

George Washington University

Georgia Institute of Technology

University of Hawai'i at Manoa

University of Illinois at Urbana-Champaign

Indiana University Bloomington

Iowa State University

Johns Hopkins University

Kent State University

University of Kentucky

University of Louisville

McMaster University

University of Maryland

University of Massachusetts Amherst

Massachusetts Institute of Technology

University of Michigan

Michigan State University

University of Minnesota

National Library of Medicine

University of Nebraska–Lincoln

University of North Carolina at Chapel Hill

North Carolina State University

Northwestern University

Ohio University

Ohio State University

University of Oklahoma

Pennsylvania State University

University of Pittsburgh

Purdue University

Rice University

University of Rochester

Southern Illinois University Carbondale

Texas A&M University

Texas Tech University

University of Virginia

Virginia Tech

University of Washington

University of Waterloo

Yale University

York University

REPRESENTATIVE DOCUMENTS

AgEcon Search

AgEcon SEARCH

RESEARCH IN AGRICULTURAL & APPLIED ECONOMICS

NEW SEARCH
Home :: Contact Us

BROWSE
➔ By institution/journal
➔ By author
➔ By date
➔ By subject category

SUBMIT
➔ Submit your paper
➔ Want to Participate?
➔ Submission Instructions
➔ Registration Instructions

HELP
➔ F.A.Q.
➔ Tips

STATISTICS
➔ Statistics 2001-2008
➔ Current Statistics

AgEcon Search >

ABOUT AGECON SEARCH

OVERVIEW

AgEcon Search: Research in Agricultural and Applied Economics collects, indexes, and electronically distributes full text copies of scholarly research in the broadly defined field of agricultural economics including sub disciplines such as agribusiness, food supply, natural resource economics, environmental economics, policy issues, agricultural trade, and economic development.

The majority of items in *AgEcon Search* are working papers, conference papers, and journal articles, although other types such as books chapters and government documents are included. *AgEcon Search* will serve as the permanent archive for this literature and encourages authors and organizations to use this electronic library as the storehouse for additional appropriate scholarly electronic works.

AgEcon Search is co-sponsored by the Department of Applied Economics and the University Libraries at University of Minnesota and the Agricultural and Applied Economics Association.

The site has received encouragement and financial support from:

Agricultural Economics Reference Organization
Agricultural and Applied Economics Association
European Association of Agricultural Economists
Farm Foundation
International Association of Agricultural Economists
USDA Economic Research Service

AgEcon Search is part of the University of Minnesota's Digital Conservancy, which provides stewardship, reliable long-term access, and broad dissemination of the digital scholarly and administrative works of the University of Minnesota faculty, departments, centers and offices.

Papers and articles downloaded from AgEcon Search may be used for non-commercial purposes and personal study only. No other use, including posting to another Internet site, is permitted without permission from the copyright owner, or as allowed under the provisions of Fair Use, U.S. Copyright Act, Title 17 U.S.C.

AgEcon Search does not hold the copyright to articles, working papers, conference papers, or other materials available in the database. Copyrights may be held by any of the following: individual authors, multiple authors, organizations, institutions, or publishers.

HISTORY

AgEcon Search began in 1995 as an experiment to see if it were possible to use the internet to archive, index and deliver on demand, full text working papers produced by university agricultural economics departments. The first papers were from agricultural economics departments at Minnesota and Wisconsin. These early papers predated the World Wide Web and were mounted on a GOPHER server in WordPerfect format. The project was (and still is) a cooperative project of the University of Minnesota Libraries, the Department of Applied Economics at the University of Minnesota and the Agricultural and Applied Economics Association (AAEA). The Farm Foundation and the Economic Research Service of the U.S. Department of Agriculture provided financial support in the beginning of the project. Patricia Rodkewich and Louise Letnes managed AgEcon Search until Patricia's retirement in 2001, when Julie Kelly joined the AgEcon Search team. Erik Biever also served on the original AgEcon Search team, providing valued technical services and guidance. The members of the Agricultural Economics Reference Organization endorsed the efforts of AgEcon Search early on and have been instrumental in expanding the use of AgEcon Search in their respective institutions.

Since its inception AgEcon Search has operated as a distributed network, with each institution designating a member of their organization to submit papers on their behalf. With this model, costs for maintaining the system were kept low and institutions do not have to pay membership fees for participation. In the cases where an institution had no central person to act as the network member, a fee has been charged for AgEcon Search staff to submit papers. The first organization to choose this option was the Agricultural and Applied Economics Association, which since 1997 has been contracting with AgEcon Search to post its annual conference papers.

ADVISORY GROUP

The *AgEcon Search* Advisory Board was initiated in 2006, to provide guidance to the project on priorities and future directions. Members include:

Rob King, chair
Professor and Department Head
University of Minnesota, Department of Applied Economics

Phil Pardey

Professor
University of Minnesota, Department of Applied Economics

Krijn Poppe
Professor
Agricultural Economics Research Institute (LEI),
Wageningen University and Research Centre, The Netherlands

Linda Eells and Julie Kelly
Co-coordinators, AgEcon Search
Ex officio members

PERSONNEL

AgEcon Search is maintained at the University of Minnesota, with responsibility shared between the University Libraries and the Department of Applied Economics. Day to day operations are carried out by the co-coordinators:

Linda Eells
Librarian, Waite Library, Department of Applied Economics

Julie Kelly
Librarian, Magrath Library, University Libraries

ADDING YOUR PAPERS TO *AGECON SEARCH*

We welcome working papers, conference papers, journals, and other materials from academic departments, professional societies, government agencies, and non-government organizations. Please write the coordinators at aesearch@umn.edu. We will set up a section for your group, and give you instructions about how to begin submitting papers.

There are no costs for posting papers for groups who designate one person to fill out the submission forms and upload papers. There are small charges per paper for groups that have each author submit their own papers, or have staff at the University of Minnesota do the input. For more information contact the coordinators at aesearch@umn.edu.

If your group has papers that need to be digitized, the coordinators can help you with that process, or arrange to have it done for a fee.

Journals included in AgEcon Search

Groups contributing papers to AgEcon Search

AgEcon Search in Print

Go to the AgEcon Search home page

AgEcon SEARCH

RESEARCH IN AGRICULTURAL & APPLIED ECONOMICS

NEW SEARCH

Home :: Contact Us

BROWSE
- By institution/journal
- By author
- By date
- By subject category

SUBMIT
- Submit your paper
- Want to Participate?
- Submission Instructions
- Registration Instructions

HELP
- F.A.Q.
- Tips

STATISTICS
- Statistics 2001-2008
- Current Statistics

AgEcon Search >

AGECON SEARCH FAQ

What is AgEcon Search?
What types of materials are included in AgEcon Search?
How can I contact AgEcon Search?
Are there any costs involved in searching AgEcon Search? In submitting papers?
How do I sign up to receive weekly e-mail updates listing selected new papers?
Are papers in AgEcon Search peer-reviewed?
Do you accept only English language working papers?
If my working paper or conference paper later evolves into a journal article, will the publisher be OK with having an earlier version on AgEcon Search?
What should I do to get my department or organization started submitting papers to AgEcon Search?
How do I suggest other working paper series, conferences, or journals that might be included in AgEcon Search?
What formats do you accept?
What institutions have their papers on AgEcon Search?
What software does AgEcon Search use?
What journals are included in AgEcon Search -- and how can I link directly to them?
What is AgNIC?
How can I read the papers in AgEcon Search?
I've downloaded Adobe Reader software, but I still can't open the PDF files. Help?

What is AgEcon Search?

AgEcon Search is a free-to-user Web site that contains the full text of working papers, conference papers and journal articles in applied economics, including the subtopics of agricultural, consumer, energy, environmental, and resource economics. Contributors include academic institutions, government agencies, professional associations, and non-government organizations.

AgEcon Search is maintained at the University of Minnesota by the Dept. of Applied Economics and University Libraries, and the Agricultural and Applied Economics Association is also a main sponsor.

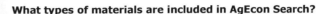

What types of materials are included in AgEcon Search?

The great majority of items in AgEcon Search are of working papers, conference papers and journal articles, although it does include book chapters, books, theses, dissertations, reports, government documents, Plan B Masters papers, and appendices to journal articles. Other types of documents will also be considered. All are in PDF format.

How can I contact AgEcon Search?

Our e-mail address is aesearch@umn.edu. Our mailing address is AgEcon Search, Waite Library, Dept. of Applied Economics, University of Minnesota, 1994 Buford Ave, St. Paul MN 55108-6040, USA. The phone number of Waite Library is 612-625-1705.

Are there any costs involved in searching AgEcon Search? In submitting papers?

There are no costs involved in searching, viewing, or downloading material from AgEcon Search.

There are no costs for posting papers for groups who designate one person to fill out the submission forms and upload papers. There are small charges per paper for groups that have each author submit their own papers, or have staff at the University of Minnesota do the input. For more information contact the coordinators at aesearch@umn.edu.

If your group has papers that need to be digitized, the coordinators can help you with that process, or arrange to have it done for a fee.

How do I sign up to receive weekly e-mail updates listing selected new papers?

E-mail updates are sent out about once a week. Anyone can sign up for this free service.

Are papers in AgEcon Search peer-reviewed?

All papers in AgEcon Search are part of a series or conference or journal sponsored by one of the participating organizations, and each group has a review mechanism. The procedures vary, and details can be obtained by contacting the sponsoring organization.

Do you accept only English language working papers?

We happily take papers in languages other than English. We do ask that you include an English title and abstract.

If my working paper or conference paper later evolves into a journal article, will the publisher be OK with having an earlier version on AgEcon Search?

With rare exception, publishers of journals in the fields covered in

AgEcon Search are fine with having earlier reports of a project in the form of a working paper or conference paper available on the Web. To prevent confusion, you might consider changing the title of the paper before submitting it to a journal.

What should I do to get my department or organization started submitting papers to AgEcon Search?

Just write the coordinators at aesearch@umn.edu. We will set up a section for your group, and give you instructions about how to begin submitting papers. If you would like us to do any of the submitting for you, we can discuss the options and costs.

How do I suggest other working paper series, conferences, or journals that might be included in AgEcon Search?

Drop us a note at aesearch@umn.edu.

What formats do you accept?

Currently, all papers in AgEcon Search are in PDF format.

What institutions have their papers on AgEcon Search?

Check the list of institutions.

What software does AgEcon Search use?

AgEcon Search runs on DSpace software, which is open source, and was jointly developed by MIT Libraries and Hewlett-Packard Labs

What journals are included in AgEcon Search -- and how can I link directly to them?

Check the list of journals , which includes URLs for directly linking to each journal.

What is AgNIC?

AgNIC, http://www.agnic.org/, is the Agriculture Network Information Center -- a voluntary alliance working to offer reliable access to quality agricultural information and sources. The University of Minnesota is responsible for the agricultural economics portion of AgNIC. To suggest resources to be included in AgNIC, send a note to aesearch@umn.edu.

How can I read the papers in AgEcon Search?

All papers in AgEcon Search are in Adobe Acrobat Portable Document Format (PDF). You can download the free Adobe Reader software at: http://www.adobe.com/products/acrobat /readstep2.html. If you have trouble opening a particular PDF file, try switching to a different Web browser (i.e. Internet Explorer or Mozilla Firefox).

I've downloaded Adobe Reader software, but I still can't open the PDF files. Help?

Check another PDF file from another source to see if you are able

to open it. If not, then you may need to check that your browser is set to recognize PDF files.

Advice from one Internet Explorer user: "...the Acrobat Helper Object got removed from the list of Internet Explorer Add-Ons, so it was not recognising .pdf files. As it happened, I was trying to download such a file from your site, but actually it affected all .pdf files. The solution was simply to re-install Acrobat Reader and that re-installed the missing Helper Object."

Go to the AgEcon Search home page

Brought to you by the University of Minnesota Department of Applied Economics and the University of Minnesota Libraries with cooperation from the Agricultural and Applied Economics Association.

All papers are in Acrobat (.pdf) format. Get Adobe Reader

Contact Us

Powered by:

AgEcon Search: Research in Agricultural and Applied Economics
http://ageconsearch.umn.edu/

Report to the AAEA Board
December 17, 2012

Executive Summary

AgEcon Search has nearly 60,000 papers (up from about 48,000 a year ago) from over 250 organizations in 30 countries, including 65 journals.

This year we have had the opportunity to add a number of older publications, including Choices, that were not available in digital format, and to further explore the idea of hosting research data. We have also focused on recruiting material from a broader range of countries, and were lucky to have some support for all of those activities.

A highlight of the year was receiving the AAEA President's Award.

Full Report

Outreach, Collaboration, Initiatives

In service to AAEA, we continue to write material for the Exchange, host the Selected Papers and Posters from the Annual Conference, work with the Outreach Committee, staff an exhibit at the Annual Conference, and promote the organization through our regular activities.

In August 2012, AgEcon Search had a booth at the International Association of Agricultural Economists meeting in Brazil. This gave us an opportunity to promote AgEcon Search, including AAEA's role, as well as make contacts with many potential contributors.

In 2011 we began a pilot project with AARES to host data from published research projects of their members. We are utilizing Dataverse, the free, hosted software designed for social sciences data. The site may be found at http://dvn.iq.harvard.edu/dvn/dv/AARES. In 2012 WAEA also expressed an interest in having a similar site, and we are in the process of setting that up.

AARES was also interested in having the papers from earlier conferences scanned from microfiche and added to AgEcon Search. We are in the process of that project and expect to finish in early 2013.

After approaching ERS about possibly digitizing their ceased publication, Journal of Agricultural Economics Research, we learned that they had quite a few series of research reports that were scanned but not yet uploaded. We have obtained copies and are in the process of adding them to AgEcon Search.

New Resources

New groups/journals submitting their papers to AgEcon Search in 2012 include:

- Acta Oeconomica et Informatica
- AFBM Journal
- AgLetter
- Amber Waves
- Crawford Fund

    ☐ Food Research Institute Studies
    ☐ Henry A. Wallace Institute for Alternative Agriculture
    ☐ Institut National de la Recherche Agronomique (INRA)
    ☐ Instituto Nacional de Investigaci☐n Agropecuaria (INIA)
    ☐ Journal of Agricultural Economics Research
    ☐ Journal of Regional Analysis and Policy
    ☐ Land and Water Forum
    ☐ Serbian Association of Agricultural Economists
    ☐ Sociedad Uruguaya de Economistas Agr'colas (SUEA)
    ☐ St. Olaf College
    ☐ Structure and Performance of Agriculture and Agri-products Industry (SPAA)
    ☐ University of California-Davis, Center for Cooperatives
    ☐ University of Stirling
    ☐ University of Vermont
    ☐ University of Weihenstephan-Triesdorf
    ☐ Wheat Studies

Growth and use

As of December 1, 2012:

    Number of papers: 59,360
    Papers added in the last 12 months: 10,816

Use of the AAEA papers continues to be very high.

	Number of Papers/Posters	Downloads in the last 24 months
1997 AAEA Meeting	9	1,023
1998 AAEA Meeting	246	29,723
1999 AAEA Meeting	239	36,620
2000 AAEA Meeting	171	22,005
2001 AAEA Meeting	342	57,129
2002 AAEA Meeting	327	42,948
2003 AAEA Meeting	370	56,688
2004 AAEA Meeting	516	86,428
2005 AAEA Meeting	468	71,902
2006 AAEA Meeting	452	83,857
2007 AAEA Meeting	346	63,077
2008 AAEA Meeting	290	72,511
2009 AAEA Meeting	290	58,434
2010 AAEA Meeting	612	96,890
2011 AAEA Meeting	574	115,742
2012 AAEA Meeting	575	41,763 (8 months)
Policy Issues	12	883
Choices (1986-2012)	1381	32,378

A major milestone this year was scanning and uploading the older issues of Choices that were previously only available in print, 1986-2002.

Support

AAEA generously provides funds to AgEcon Search, covering the exhibit at the annual meeting, some travel expenses and the personnel to add conference papers to the database. Other groups also contributed to the project during the last year:

- The CME Foundation gave us a grant for $12,000 to digitize and upload two ceased journals from Stanford's Food Research Institute (Food Research Institute Studies and Wheat Studies). The project is nearly complete.

- The National Agricultural Library extended the small grant we received in 2011, allowing us to continue digitizing older working papers we obtained from UC-Berkeley.

- The University of Minnesota Libraries awarded us a $3,000 grant to cover student expenses for uploading copies of papers that were already in digital format but were not held in a repository.

- AAEA covered the scanning and uploading costs for making the print-only volumes of Choices (1986-2002) available.

- IAAE provided travel funds and waived our expenses to have an exhibit at their meeting in Brazil.

- AARES provided travel funds and provided booth space for us at their 2012 meeting in Fremantle, and this allowed us to make progress on our data archiving project.

- University of Minnesota Department of Applied Economics and the University Libraries provided travel funding as well as in kind support for librarian and computer professional salaries, student salaries, supplies, hardware, and software.

- A University of Minnesota Libraries team provides technical support for AgEcon Search as needed, and the group includes a Web application developer, a Web designer, and the manager of the Libraries' Digital Library Services group.

In 2012, the AgEcon Search Special Purpose Fund was chartered at the AAEA meeting so we will be able to begin utilizing proceeds from the fund next year.

On the Horizon

A move to a new software platform will be finalized in 2013.

In order to make the journal articles even more easily accessible, we hope to arrange for DOIs (digital object identifiers) for each article.

We will offer the possibility of hosting data in Dataverse to additional groups in the upcoming year.

In an effort to include more research produced in the developing world, we are negotiating with journals from Ethiopia, Nigeria, and Pakistan and hope to be adding them soon.

PubMed Central®

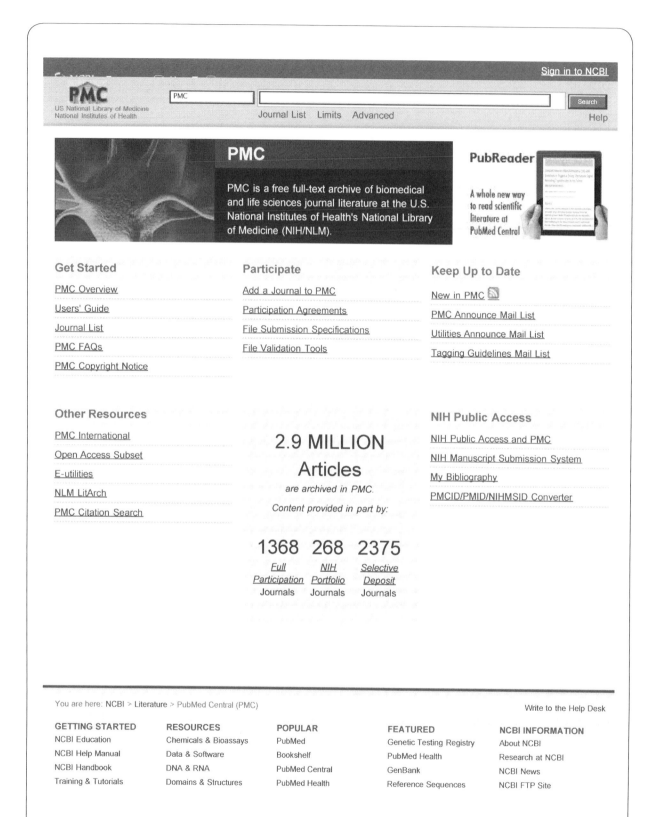

PMC Overview

PubMed Central® (PMC) is a free archive of biomedical and life sciences journal literature at the U.S. National Institutes of Health's National Library of Medicine (NIH/NLM). In keeping with NLM's legislative mandate to collect and preserve the biomedical literature, PMC serves as a digital counterpart to NLM's extensive print journal collection. Launched in February 2000, PMC was developed and is managed by NLM's National Center for Biotechnology Information (NCBI).

Free Access: A Core Principle of PMC

As an archive, PMC is designed to provide permanent access to all of its content, even as technology evolves and current digital literature formats potentially become obsolete. NLM believes that the best way to ensure the accessibility and viability of digital material over time is through consistent and active use of the archive. For this reason, free access to all of its journal literature is a core principle of PMC.

Please note, however, that free access does not mean that there is no copyright protection. As described on our copyright page publishers and individual authors continue to hold copyright on the material in PMC and users must abide by the terms defined by the copyright holder.

How Journal Articles are Provided to PMC

PMC is a repository for journal literature deposited by participating publishers, as well as for author manuscripts that have been submitted in compliance with the Public Access Policy mandated by NIH and similar policies of other research funding agencies. PMC is not a publisher and does not publish journal articles itself.

PMC offers publishers a number of ways in which to participate and deposit their content in the archive. Although free access is a requirement, publishers can delay the release of their material in PMC for a reasonable period after publication. Publishers may also obtain a copy of their deposit material at any time, at no cost.

PMC's Integration with other Resources

In addition to its role as an archive, the value of PMC lies in its capacity to store and cross-reference data from diverse sources using a common format within a single repository. With PMC, a user can quickly search the entire collection of full-text articles and locate all relevant material. PMC also allows for the integration of its literature with a variety of other information resources that can enhance the research and knowledge fields of scientists, clinicians and others.

International Collaboration and Durability

NLM is collaborating internationally with other agencies that share the goals of PMC. Maintaining copies of PMC's literature in other reliable international archives that operate on the same principles provides greater protection against damage or loss of the material. At the same time, the diversity of sites allows for the possibility of more and even greater innovation, ensuring the permanence of PMC over the long-term.

You are here: NCBI > Literature > PubMed Central (PMC) > PMC Overview   Write to the Help Desk

GETTING STARTED	RESOURCES	POPULAR	FEATURED	NCBI INFORMATION
NCBI Education	Chemicals & Bioassays	PubMed	Genetic Testing Registry	About NCBI
NCBI Help Manual	Data & Software	Bookshelf	PubMed Health	Research at NCBI
NCBI Handbook	DNA & RNA	PubMed Central	GenBank	NCBI News
Training & Tutorials	Domains & Structures	PubMed Health	Reference Sequences	NCBI FTP Site

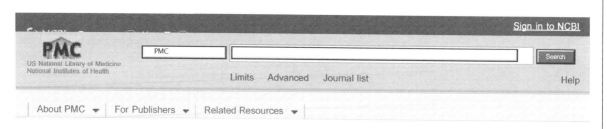

File Submission Specifications

PMC's mission is to both provide access to journal content and maintain a high-quality archive of this content over the long-term. With this in mind, PMC has designed the following sets of requirements for file submission

PMC Requires:

1. <u>XML Coding</u>: A separate XML data file for the full text of each article.
2. <u>Images</u>: The original high-resolution digital image files for all figures in each article.
3. <u>PDF</u>: A PDF file for each article.
4. <u>Supplementary Data</u>: Spreadsheets, video files, etc. available with the article.
5. <u>Delivery</u>: Files must be named and packaged for PMC.

1. XML Coding (more details)

For details on data elements and XML structure, please see the Journal Publishing DTD at http://dtd.nlm.nih.gov/publishing. For detailed information on using the Journal Publishing DTD for submissions to PMC, please read the PMC Tagging Guidelines. Please check the XML Coding Specifications for a brief overview of tagging Selective Deposit, NIH Portfolio, license statements, and release-delays.

Required Data Elements

Certain data elements must be present and used consistently in each XML or SGML file deposited in PMC, even if the corresponding DTD does not require them. These elements contribute to making the XML/SGML files self-documenting and more portable for archival purposes:

- Journal ISSN
- Journal ID or Journal title abbreviation
- Journal Publisher
- Copyright statement, where applicable
- Volume, issue (if applicable), and article sequence number or pagination
- Issue publication date
- Article electronic publication date

Additional information on tagging Selective Deposit, NIH Portfolio, Release Dates, Open Access, and Limited Access is located on the XML Coding Specifications page.

2. Images (more details)

Generally, Authors submit raw image data files to a publishing house in various formats (ppt, pdf, tif, jpg, xml, etc.). The files are then normalized to produce print or electronic output. PMC requires the normalized output, which is high-resolution, and of sufficient width and quality to be considered archival. Images generated at low resolution for display purposes are not acceptable.

Specific details on Figure, Equation, and Table Image Quality can be found on the Image Quality Specifications page.

3. PDFs

A separate PDF which directly corresponds to the individual XML or SGML data file should be provided for each book review and/or letter.

If print quality PDFs are available, please submit them. If the journal is not printed, the resolution of the images in the PDF should be no less than: Line Art 800 dpi, Halftones 300 dpi, Color 600 dpi. All fonts used in the file need to be fully embedded. Compression for images should be lossless (zip) or highest-quality JPEG. Illustrations should be encoded as vector data with no erroneous conversion to bitmaps.

4. Supplementary Data

PMC requires all available supplementary material to be submitted in a portable format, such as PDF, .doc, .csv, etc. Supplementary material should not be externally linked to a www location from the article text as a substitute for submission. Supplementary material has been defined to include all of the following:

- Voluminous material that was used to support the conclusions of the narrative, such as a genomic database or the multiple data sets for an article that presents the highlights, which can never accompany a paper based on sheer mass.

- "Extra" tables that do not display with the work, but that record the measurements on which the article is based, for example, that need to be available so the peer reviewers can check the article.

- Material added to the work for enhancement purposes, such as a quiz, an instructional video, the 3-minute version of the reaction that was described in the work with narrative and a few still images, a form that can be filled out, etc.

Video

- PMC expects good quality video, and will downsample for web streaming if necessary.

- If the meaning of the video is not clear due to low quality, it must be improved prior to submission.

- Preferred Settings:

    - Audio codec: AAC

    - Sample audio bit rate: 128 kbit/s

    - Video codec: H.264

    - Video resolution: 480 vertical lines or better

    - Format: MPEG-4 (mp4) container

- Accepted formats: (mov, avi, mpg, mpeg, mp4, mkv, flv, wmv).

- Video files larger than 1GB should be split to several episodes, each less then 1GB.

5. Delivery (more details)

PMC requires that data is named and packaged in a compressed archive, such as a zip file, to ensure that the data can be processed by our automated system. Naming Article Data Files, Naming ZIP File Packages, Revised or Corrected ZIP Files, and ZIP File Delivery are discussed on this page.

You are here: NCBI > Literature > PubMed Central (PMC) > File Submission Specifications   Write to the Help Desk

GETTING STARTED	RESOURCES	POPULAR	FEATURED	NCBI INFORMATION
NCBI Education	Chemicals & Bioassays	PubMed	Genetic Testing Registry	About NCBI
NCBI Help Manual	Data & Software	Bookshelf	PubMed Health	Research at NCBI
NCBI Handbook	DNA & RNA	PubMed Central	GenBank	NCBI News
Training & Tutorials	Domains & Structures	PubMed Health	Reference Sequences	NCBI FTP Site
	Genes & Expression	BLAST	Gene Expression Omnibus	NCBI on Facebook
	Genetics & Medicine	Nucleotide	Map Viewer	NCBI on Twitter
	Genomes & Maps	Genome	Human Genome	NCBI on YouTube
	Homology	SNP	Mouse Genome	

PMC National Advisory Committee

The PubMed Central National Advisory Committee advises the Director, NIH, the Director, NLM, and the Director, NCBI, on the content and operation of the PubMed Central repository. It is responsible for monitoring the evolution of PubMed Central and ensuring that it remains responsive to the needs of researchers, publishers, librarians and the general public. The committee meets at least once a year at the National Library of Medicine. Committee members are appointed by the NIH Director from the biomedical and information communities and the general public.

Minutes of earlier meetings

- June 27, 2013 PDF (179K).
- June 19, 2012 PDF (200K).
- June 17, 2011 PDF (192K).
- June 4, 2010 PDF (220K).
- June 15, 2009 PDF (107k).
- June 17, 2008 PDF (37k).
- April 19, 2007 PDF (36k).
- October 26, 2006 PDF (52k).
- April 26, 2006 PDF (37k).
- October 20, 2005 PDF (38k).
- April 28, 2005 PDF (27k).
- November 22, 2004 PDF (27k).
- May 10, 2004 PDF (22k).
- December 2, 2003 PDF (32k).
- June 25, 2003 PDF (26k).
- January 16, 2003 PDF (25k).
- January 14, 2002 PDF (25k).
- March 21, 2001 PDF (24k).

Committee Members

A member's term on the committee runs through the date shown alongside the member's name.

Chair: THIBODEAU, Patricia, M.L.S., M.B.A. (01/31/15)
Associate Dean for Library Services and Archives
Duke University Medical Center Library
10 Searle Drive, 103 Mudd Building
Durham, NC 27710

ANDERSON, Ivy, M.L.S. (01/31/14)
Director, Collection Development and Management
California Digital Library

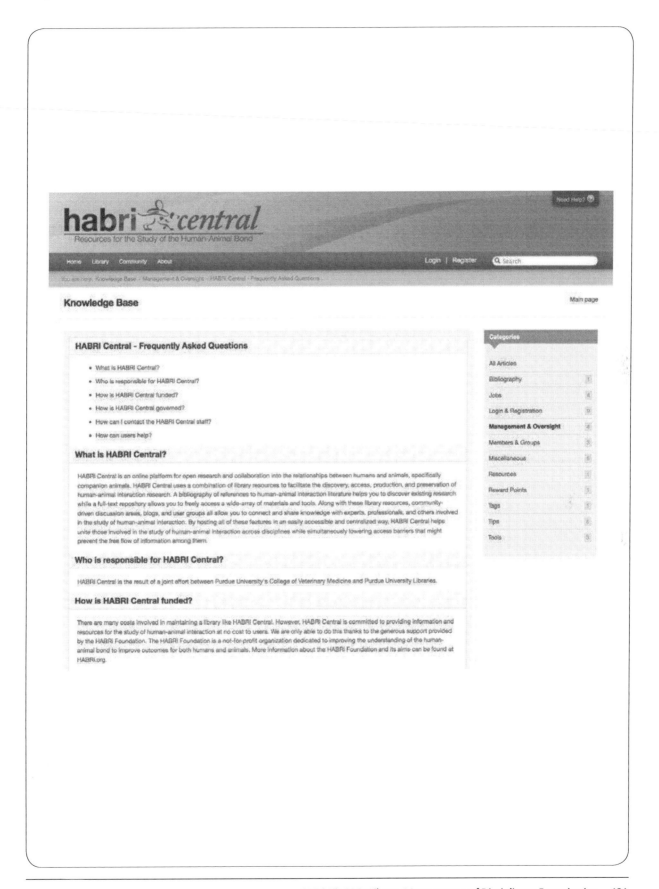

How is HABRI Central governed?

HABRI Central receives input and guidance from two different advisory boards to develop and maintain its editorial policies and to guide its operation.

Management Advisory Board

While HABRI Central is operated by staff at Purdue University, it receives additional guidance through a board of individuals involved in academia, medicine, industry, and other areas related to human-animal interaction. The Management Advisory Board convenes twice per year to discuss issues that affect the operation and sustainability of HABRI Central. Within the Management Advisory Board, seats are reserved for the chair of the HABRI Foundation's Research Workgroup, the project manager of HABRI Central, and the chair of the Editorial Board.

Editorial Board

HABRI Central's editorial policy is governed by an editorial board of experts and professionals from various fields related to human-animal interaction. The HABRI Central Editorial Board meets regularly to discuss the editorial scope of the site's content. The Pets & People book series, while associated with HABRI Central, has a separate editorial board composed of members of the Steering Committee on Human-Animal Interactions of the AVMA.

How can I contact the HABRI Central staff?

HABRI Central is based at Purdue University in Stewart Center, Room 370, 504 W State St, West Lafayette, IN 47907. For specific inquiries, please use the following email addresses:

- General information, administrator@habricentral.org
- Help & support, support@habricentral.org
- Repository content & policies, repository@habricentral.org
- Bibliography content & policies, bibliography@habricentral.org
- Tags & the controlled vocabulary, taxonomy@habricentral.org

How can users help?

HABRI Central depends on its users to maintain coverage of all areas of human-animal interaction. Without your help, we cannot provide a comprehensive survey of human-animal interaction—there are simply too many people working among too many different disciplines for one group to cover it all. By submitting your work to the repository, sharing of your opinions in the forum, or by collaborating with others through our groups, your participation is essential to building and sharing a broad understanding of human-animal interaction with others. Whether you are a veterinarian, a nurse, a shelter worker, a government official, a teacher, a pet owner, a student, or a scholar, your unique perspective is invaluable to the community. By sharing it with others through HABRI Central, you will be helping to improve everyone's understanding of the countless ways in which animals and people affect each others' lives.

Last updated @ 04:10 PM on 13 Oct 2013

0 👍   0 👎

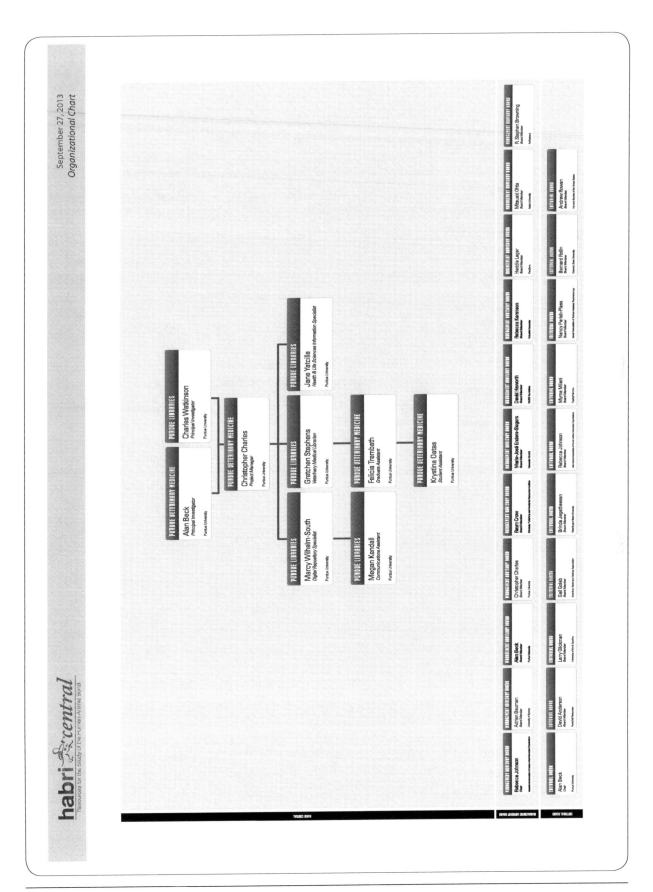

The HABRI Designated Community

HABRI Central will be aimed at diverse, international audience comprising academic researchers, practitioner experts in both human and animal health, government and non-government officials involved in handling the social implications of human-animal interaction, and the wider public – many of whom are recognized to be highly-involved and interested in these issues. One characteristic of human-animal bond studies is that there are many people engaged in activities such as animal-assisted therapy on a volunteer basis, and the business model adopted for HABRI Central needs to enable the information provided to be open to the interested lay public. Currently this information is widely dispersed and often behind subscription walls. HABRI Central, when possible, acts as an Open Access resource, with the majority of the site's content being immediately available, without charge, to users. Some material will be available directly in the repository, while other resources will be pointed to outside of the repository. Although some premium content may be available on an access fee basis, maximizing open accessibility will be essential to increasing the site's impact.

Subjects and Arrangement

Subjects Covered

HABRI Central aims to cover subjects related to human-animal interaction. On a more granular level, HABRI Central accepts material relating to the following:

Full coverage:

- Human-animal bond (i.e. human-animal relationships; human-animal relations; human-animal interactions; bonding, human-pet)
- Animal-assisted therapy (including equine-assisted therapy, pet therapy, therapy animals, therapy dogs, service animals, etc.)
- pet loss, grief and bereavement; animal-assisted activities (including animals in education, such as reading to therapy animals and animals in the classroom)
- Animal cruelty
- Animal rescue and animal shelters
- Animal welfare and well-being
- Animals in the liberal arts, education, and philosophy
- Anthrozoology and paleoanthrozoology
- Attitudes toward animals, including ethics in the human-animal relationship
- History and social impact of domesticated species
- Object attachment to animals/pets
- Pets and people
- Human relations with wild, non-domesticated species
- Transmissible diseases between man and animals (zoonosis)

Selective coverage:

- Animal behavior and ethology
- Animal handling
- Animal law
- Animal rights
- Animals in folklore, legends and mythology
- Animals in history and zooarchaeology
- Hunting, especially ethical issues
- Animals in the literary and visual arts, etc.

Scope of Coverage

Languages included / excluded:

Materials in all languages are accepted into HABRI Central.

Geographic coverage:

Materials from all geographic areas are accepted into HABRI Central. Initial emphasis on Anglo-American material reflects only the geographical limits of HABRI Central staff

Chronological period(s):

Interest is primarily in print or online materials published or created after 1960.

Currency / dates of publication:

Current imprints are primarily acquired. The acquisition of retrospective materials is usually to strengthen a specific area of the collection, to address new interdisciplinary research areas in which HAB researchers are engaged, or to replace missing materials, and is proportional to available funds, staffing and space (both physical and digital).

Level (popular, general academic, research, professional, etc.):

Research and professional works are included comprehensively. General academic works related to the key aspects of human-animal bond also are included when available. Popular works are included in the bibliography when their impact on the human-animal bond field or a related area is substantive. A majority of the bibliography focuses on peer-reviewed journal articles (both print and online), as well as theses, dissertations, books, book sections (chapters), videos, etc.

Acceptable Formats

A variety of digital material formats are accepted into HABRI Central for Resources.

Common file types are:

- Text: Microsoft Word, PDF, TXT, XML
- Image: GIF, JPEG, JPEG2000, TIFF
- Video: WMV, MP4, AVI, FLV, VOB, MOV
- Audio: MP3, WAV, WMA
- Web: HTML
- Other: PPT

HABRI Central is not just an access solution but a preservation solution as well; therefore we encourage the deposit of preservation formats so that your material is sustained for the long-term.

Preservation file types:

- Text: PDF, XML
- Image: TIFF
- Video: AVI
- Audio: WAV
- Web: HTML

We encourage you to deposit in a preservation format, but if this is not possible, access formats are also welcome.

Preservation format conversion can be complex; that is, there might be a presentation in PowerPoint, and a PowerPoint might be embedded with several image or video or audio files. Thus, each presentation will need to be evaluated to see what type of media are embedded before preservation actions are taken, and for this, consultation with the HABRI team might be necessary. To ask any questions regarding complex file preservation, please email our digital repository specialist.

Below is a list of the kind of material that is accepted for each resource type. If you have an older format type (eg microfilm, audiotape) that you would like to be placed into HABRI Central and you do not have the means to convert it, please send an email to our digital repository specialist and we'll consult with you to see how that can best be converted and deposited.

- Audio: MP3, WAV, WMA
- Book Sections: Microsoft Word, PDF, TXT, XML
- Books: Microsoft Word, PDF, TXT, XML
- Conference Papers: Microsoft Word, PDF, TXT, XML
- Datasets: Excel, SAS, SPSS
- Government documents: Microsoft Word, PDF, TXT, XML
- Journal articles: Microsoft Word, PDF, TXT, XML
- Magazine articles: Microsoft Word, PDF, TXT, XML
- Newspaper articles: Microsoft Word, PDF, TXT, XML
- Pamphlets: Microsoft Word, PDF, TXT, XML
- Posters: GIF, JPEG, JPEG2000, TIFF
- Presentations: GIF, JPEG, JPEG2000, TIFF, PPT, PDF
- Reports: Microsoft Word, PDF, TXT, XML
- Soft literatures: Microsoft Word, PDF, TXT, XML
- Still Images: GIF, JPEG, JPEG2000, TIFF
- Theses: Microsoft Word, PDF, TXT, XML
- Tools:
- Videos: WMV, MP4, AVI, FLV, VOB, MOV

Other Preservation/Conservation Considerations

HABRI Central aims to ensure authenticity of the items it preserves, whether the items have been published elsewhere or not. The HUBzero platform, on which HABRI Central runs, does file backups on a nightly basis.

Trustworthiness and Scholarly Nature of Materials

Material in HABRI Central aims to be of a scholarly nature. We therefore encourage the deposit of peer-reviewed articles and the like.

Use of "peer-reviewed" in HABRI Central:

Peer review is a process that most scholarly journals use to ensure that the articles they publish are the best scholarship currently available. When an article is submitted to a journal that is "peer-reviewed," the editors send the article out to a board of reviewers or other scholars in the same field (the author's peers) to have them evaluate the quality, validity and reliability of the article. This review process frequently is "blind," meaning that the reviewers or peers do not know the names or academic affiliation of the authors and the authors do not know who is reviewing their work.

To verify that a journal is peer-reviewed or refereed, one can check the journal or its website, usually in its author guidelines or instructions, or check the journal in UlrichsWeb Global Serials Directory.

In HABRI Central, the "peer-reviewed" icon indicates that the given article appears in a journal that is "peer-reviewed" as verified in UlrichsWeb Global Serials Directory or the journal itself.

We also review all material that comes into HABRI Central to ensure it adheres to the standard set forth by us.

Revision of the HABRI Central Collection Development Policy

HABRI Central is committed to maintenance, periodic review, and revision of all its policies, procedures and documentation as outlined in the Digital Preservation Policy. This Collection Policy is included in this practice. Users who wish to challenge HABRI Central's Collection Policy, or offer suggestions or comments on it may do so through the digital repository specialist. The digital repository specialist can be contacted at repository@habricentral.org.

Last updated @ 06:49 PM on 24 Sep 2012.

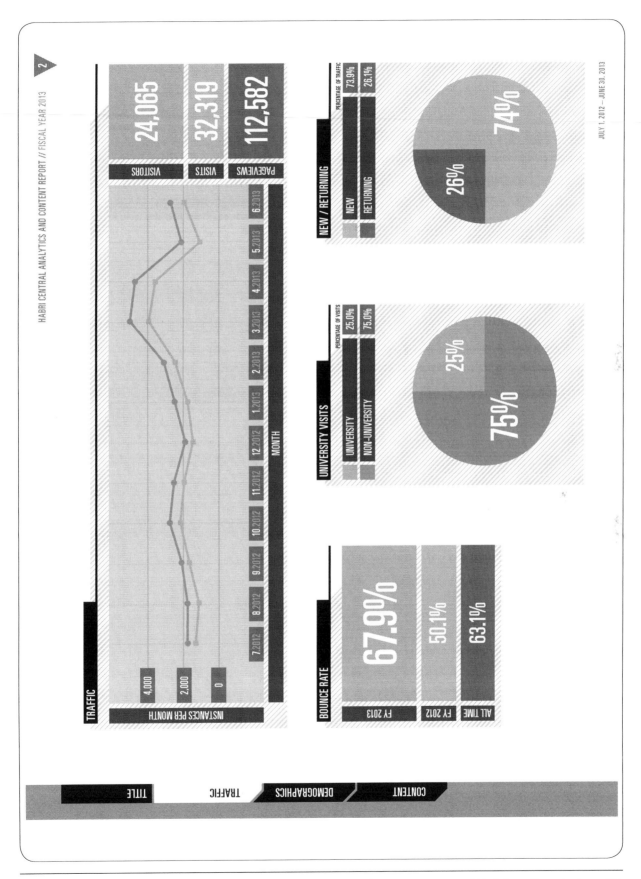

HABRI CENTRAL ANALYTICS AND CONTENT REPORT // FISCAL YEAR 2013

JULY 1, 2012 — JUNE 30, 2013

TRAFFIC

VISITORS	24,065
VISITS	32,319
PAGEVIEWS	112,582

INSTANCES PER MONTH

4,000 / 2,000 / 0

MONTH

7.2012 8.2012 9.2012 10.2012 11.2012 12.2012 1.2013 2.2013 3.2013 4.2013 5.2013 6.2013

NEW / RETURNING

PERCENTAGE OF TRAFFIC
NEW 73.9%
RETURNING 26.1%

74%
26%

UNIVERSITY VISITS

PERCENTAGE OF VISITS
UNIVERSITY 25.0%
NON-UNIVERSITY 75.0%

75%
25%

BOUNCE RATE

FY 2013 67.9%
FY 2012 50.1%
ALL TIME 63.1%

TITLE | TRAFFIC | DEMOGRAPHICS | CONTENT

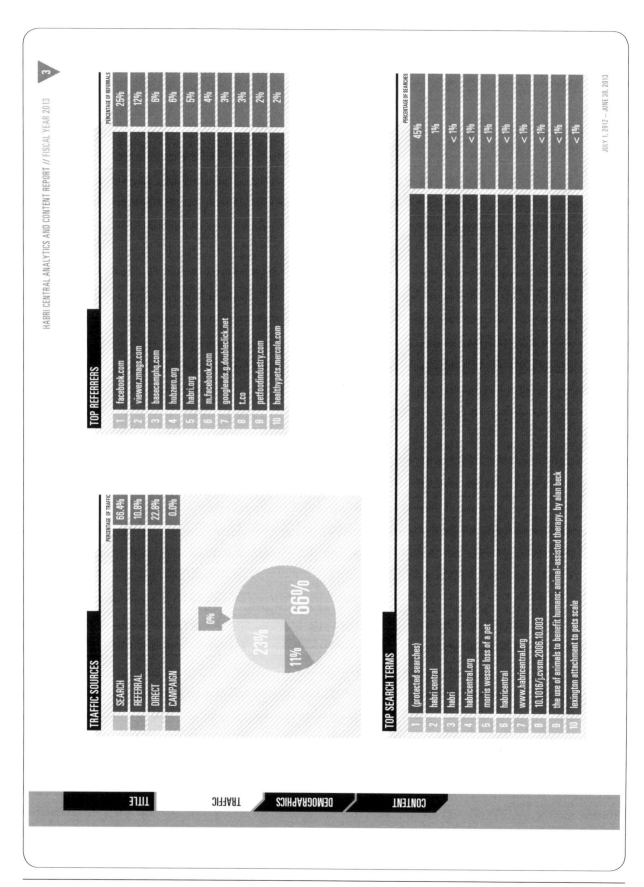

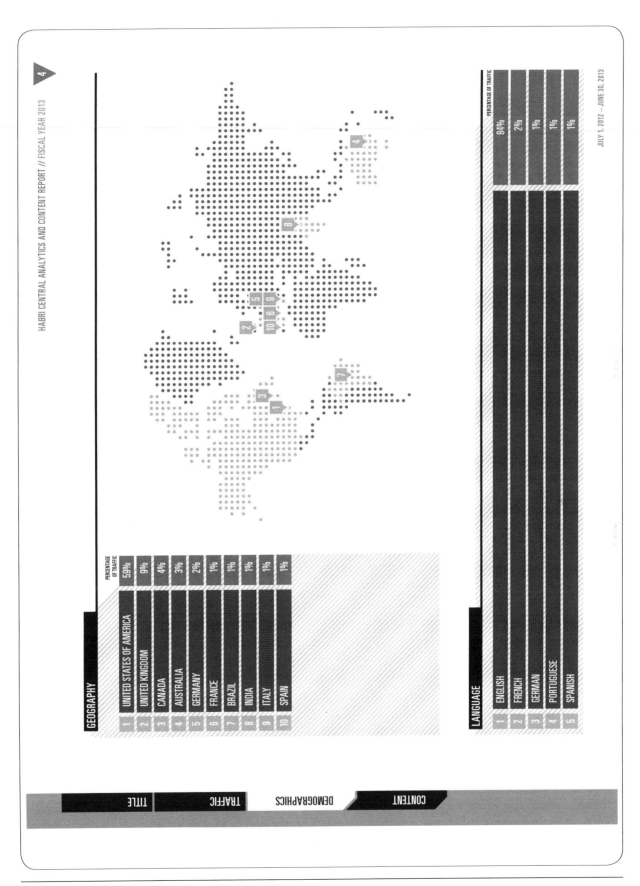

HABRI CENTRAL ANALYTICS AND CONTENT REPORT // FISCAL YEAR 2013

JULY 1, 2012 — JUNE 30, 2013

GEOGRAPHY

		PERCENTAGE OF TRAFFIC
1	UNITED STATES OF AMERICA	59%
2	UNITED KINGDOM	9%
3	CANADA	4%
4	AUSTRALIA	3%
5	GERMANY	2%
6	FRANCE	1%
7	BRAZIL	1%
8	INDIA	1%
9	ITALY	1%
10	SPAIN	1%

LANGUAGE

		PERCENTAGE OF TRAFFIC
1	ENGLISH	84%
2	FRENCH	2%
3	GERMAN	1%
4	PORTUGUESE	1%
5	SPANISH	1%

TITLE TRAFFIC DEMOGRAPHICS CONTENT

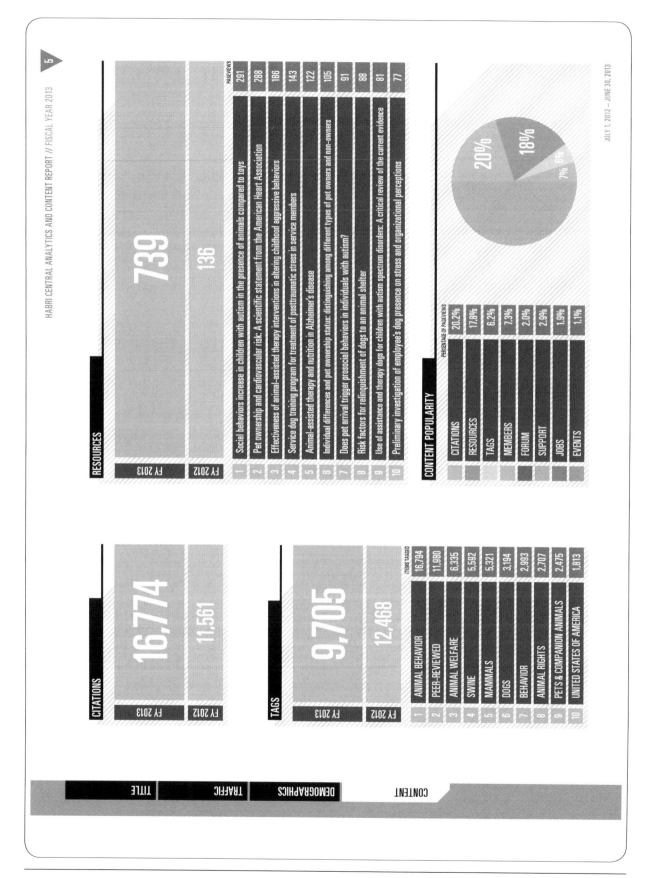

Industry Studies Working Papers

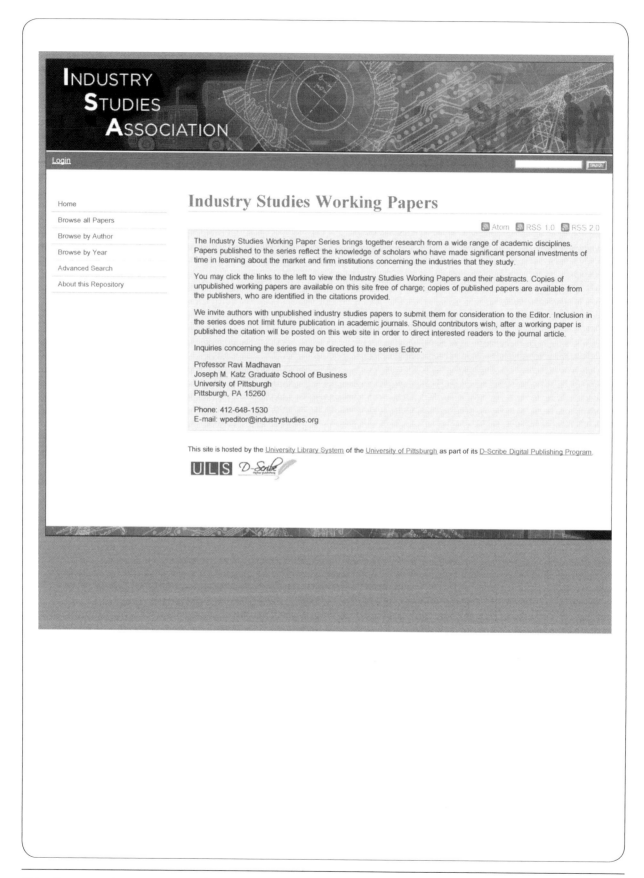

Industry Studies Working Papers

Atom · RSS 1.0 · RSS 2.0

The Industry Studies Working Paper Series brings together research from a wide range of academic disciplines. Papers published to the series reflect the knowledge of scholars who have made significant personal investments of time in learning about the market and firm institutions concerning the industries that they study.

You may click the links to the left to view the Industry Studies Working Papers and their abstracts. Copies of unpublished working papers are available on this site free of charge; copies of published papers are available from the publishers, who are identified in the citations provided.

We invite authors with unpublished industry studies papers to submit them for consideration to the Editor. Inclusion in the series does not limit future publication in academic journals. Should contributors wish, after a working paper is published the citation will be posted on this web site in order to direct interested readers to the journal article.

Inquiries concerning the series may be directed to the series Editor:

Professor Ravi Madhavan
Joseph M. Katz Graduate School of Business
University of Pittsburgh
Pittsburgh, PA 15260

Phone: 412-648-1530
E-mail: wpeditor@industrystudies.org

This site is hosted by the University Library System of the University of Pittsburgh as part of its D-Scribe Digital Publishing Program.

Home
Browse all Papers
Browse by Author
Browse by Year
Advanced Search
About this Repository

Login

InterNano

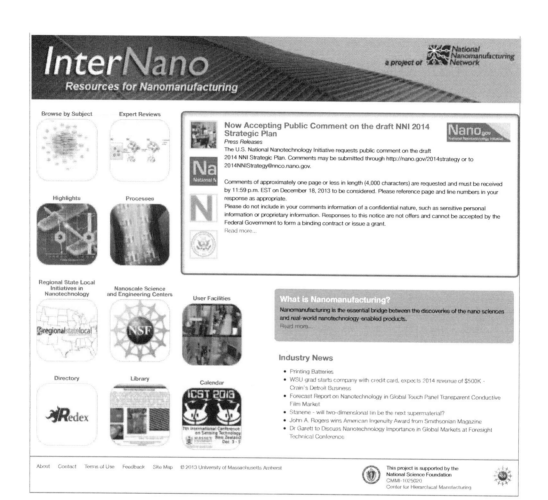

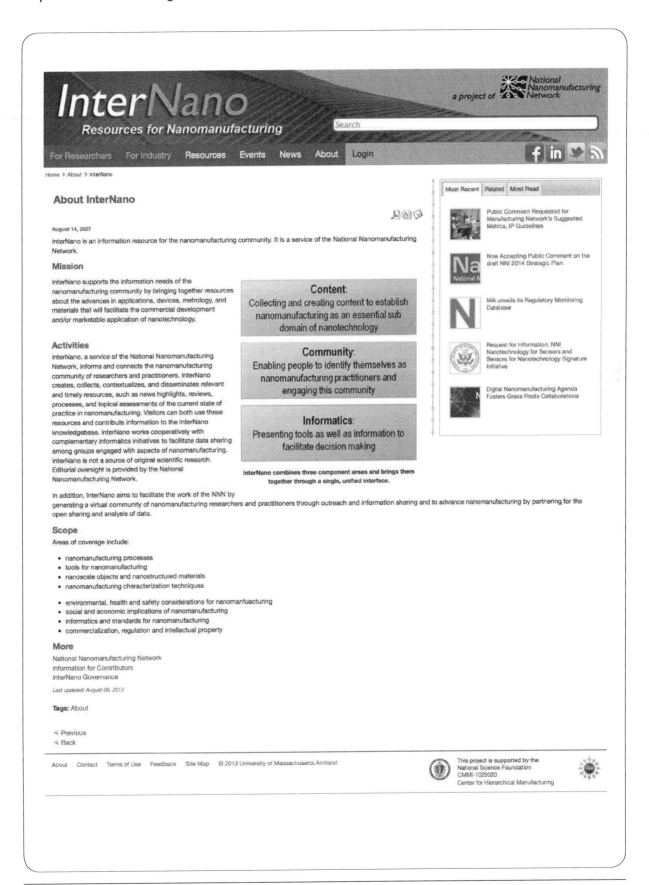

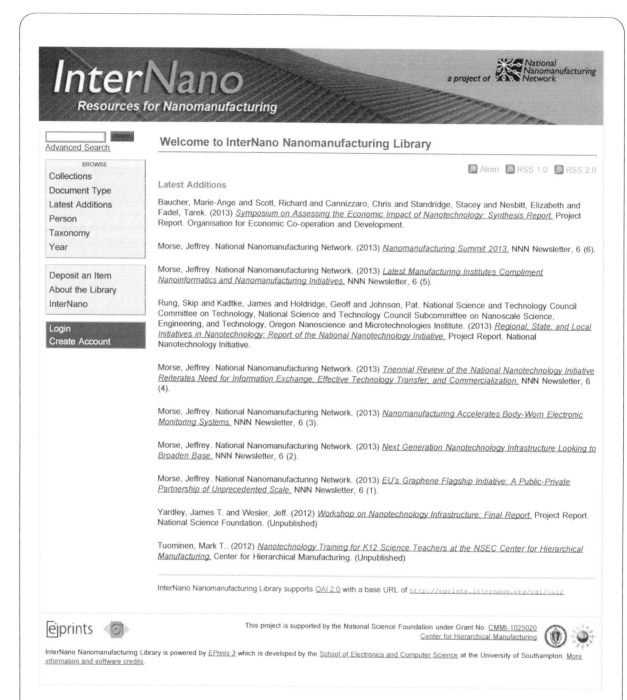

InterNano
Resources for Nanomanufacturing

a project of National Nanomanufacturing Network

| Search |
Advanced Search

BROWSE
Collections
Document Type
Latest Additions
Person
Taxonomy
Year

Deposit an Item
About the Library
InterNano

Login
Create Account

About the Library

The Internano Nanomanufacturing Library is a central digital repository of nanomanufacturing research and trade information for the nanomanfuacturing community. It is administered by the National Nanomanfuacturing Network and funded by the National Science Foundation.

Central repositories—or subject, thematic, or disciplinary repositories—bring the scholarly outputs of a single domain together to a single point of access. Examples of central repositories include arXive, RePec, e-LIS, and PubMed.

This site is powered by EPrints 3, free software developed by the University of Southampton.

Content Policy

- The InterNano Nanomanufacturing Library accepts any scientific, scholarly, or technical work relevant to the nanomanfuacturing enterprise.
- The work must be in a digital format ready for public dissemination. Works comprised of multiple files and file formats are supported.
- Suitable works include pre-prints (pre-refereed journal papers), post-prints (post-refereed journal papers), conference papers or posters, presentations, technical papers, reports and working papers, books and book chapters, newspaper and magazine articles, newsletters, and data.
- All submissions are approved by the repository staff before being posted.

Copyright

The inclusion of works in the InterNano Nanomanufacturing Library is an extension of an author's copyright to the work. Authors are responsible for clearing any copyright restrictions on the elecronic distribution of their work. SHERPA/RoMEO is a searchable database of publisher's copyright and self-archiving policies.

More about copyright, author rights, and open access....

Deposit Agreement

To ensure that works are submitted in accordance with copyright law, InterNano includes a click-through deposit agreement to declare responsiblity for copyright. The language of that agreement is included here for your convenience.

For work being deposited by its own author:

In self-archiving this collection of files and associated bibliographic metadata, I grant InterNano the right to store them and to make them permanently available publicly for free on-line. I declare that this material is my own intellectual property and I understand that InterNano does not assume any responsibility if there is any breach of copyright in distributing these files or metadata. (All authors are urged to prominently assert their copyright on the title page of their work.)

InterNano recommends Creative Commons licenses for authors who wish to assert copyright and promote further use of their work.

For work being deposited by someone other than its author:

I hereby declare that the collection of files and associated bibliographic metadata that I am archiving at InterNano is in the public domain. If this is not the case, I accept full responsibility for any breach of copyright that distributing these files or metadata may entail.

Preservation

InterNano is intended to be a permanent record of the nanomanfuacturing enterprise. It is the responsibility of InterNano to preserve submitted content using accepted preservation standards and techniques.

Authors may request to add updated documents to a work's record; posting updated versions along with the original material is the preferred way to show the progress of research.

A work may be removed at the author's request or if it is found to fall outside of the scope of the repository. A work may also be removed if it is found to violate copyright law. When it is necessary to remove a work, a placeholder will be left behind to inform readers that the content has been deliberately withdrawn.

Support

InterNano repository staff are available to assist with the uploading of works to the repository. Contact internano@internano.org for general questions, questions about copyright and open access, or technical assistance.

 eprints

This project is supported by the National Science Foundation under Grant No. CMMI-1025020
Center for Hierarchical Manufacturing

InterNano Nanomanufacturing Library is powered by EPrints 3 which is developed by the School of Electronics and Computer Science at the University of Southampton. More information and software credits.

InterNano Advisory Board

Overview

The National Nanomanufacturing Network (NNN) is an alliance of academic, government and industry partners that cooperate to advance nanomanufacturing strength in the U.S. As part of its mission, the NNN offers a digital library and information clearinghouse service to the academic, industrial, and government stakeholders in nanomanufacturing.

Mission and Objectives:

The mission of InterNano is to support the nanomanufacturing research and development community as a comprehensive service that collects, organizes, and distributes information for and about the nanomanufacturing domain.

To obtain its goal of becoming the premier information service for the nanomanufacturing community, InterNano will:

- Provide directories and databases of nanomanufacturing processes and nanostructured materials properties

- Offer a standardized vocabulary for resource discovery and domain definition

- Make timely educational materials, workshop reports, and nanomanufacturing events information publicly available

- Facilitate networking and information exchange between nanomanufacturing community members

- Increase exposure to scientific literature being published in nanomanufacturing

- Aggregate publicly available information (news, events, job listings, grant opportunities)

- Curate collections of domain-specific products, including images

Advisory Board Role

The Advisory Board will:

- Serve as a focus group for InterNano feature and content development;
- Be available as resources for contacts and domain expertise;
- Advocate InterNano within members' communities;
- Identify new opportunity areas for added value development of InterNano.

Membership to the Advisory Board requests a one-year, renewable commitment; members will be listed on the InterNano web site.

The advisory board will confer three to four times per year via conference call or web-based meeting for updates and discussion. The advisory board will provide feedback and advice to the steering committee and project team on these occasions, and informally throughout the year.

State and national academic researchers, federal research officials, and industry partners will constitute the board.

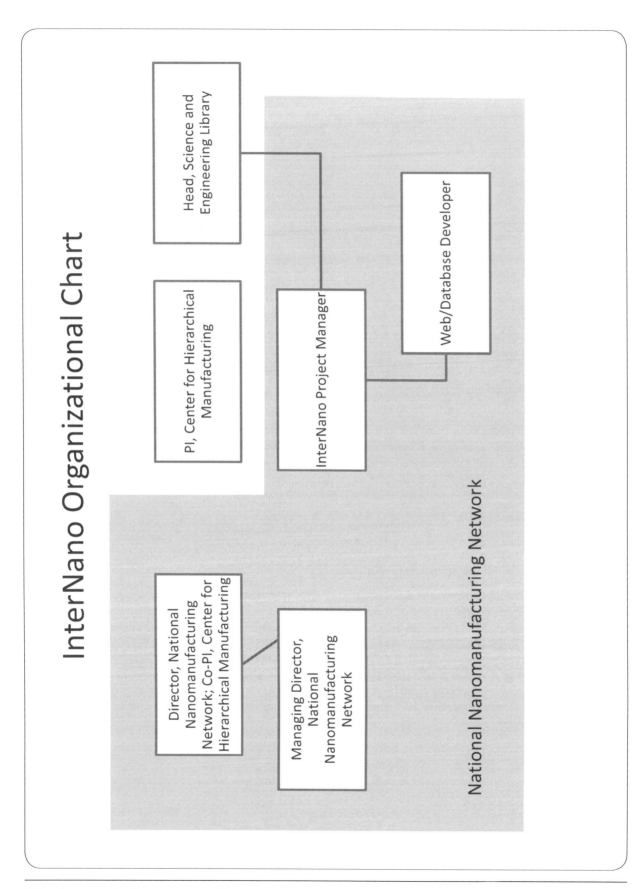

InterNano Organizational Chart

Head, Science and Engineering Library

PI, Center for Hierarchical Manufacturing

InterNano Project Manager

Web/Database Developer

Director, National Nanomanufacturing Network; Co-PI, Center for Hierarchical Manufacturing

Managing Director, National Nanomanufacturing Network

National Nanomanufacturing Network

The Aphasiology Archive

The Aphasiology Archive
University Library System, University of Pittsburgh

Home || About || Browse || Search || Help

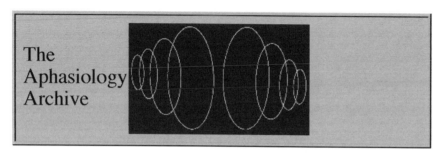
The Aphasiology Archive

Welcome to The Aphasiology Archive.

Search the Titles, Abstracts and Keywords: [   ]   [Search]

- **Browse** - Browse the archive by **Conference Year**
- **Simple Search** - Search the archive using the most common fields.
- **Advanced Search** - Search the archive using a more complex range of fields.

At present, The Aphasiology Archive contains 1734 documents

Clinical Aphasiology Conference Web Site

Running on *GNU EPrints* archive-creating software, which generates eprints archives that are compliant with the Open Archives Protocol for Metadata Harvesting OAI 1.1 and 2.0.
The eprints.org archive-creating software is available for free at http://www.eprints.org/.

Site Administrator: aphasiology@mail.pitt.edu

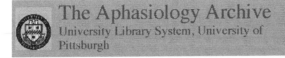

The Aphasiology Archive
University Library System, University of Pittsburgh

Home || About || Browse || Search || Help

About this archive

Welcome to The Aphasiology Archive a repository of papers presented at the Clinical Aphasiology Conference (CAC). Since 1971, the Clinical Aphasiology Conference has provided an important forum for the exchange of information related to diagnosis, assessment, and treatment of persons with communication impairments - primarily those of aphasia but also including a restricted range of related disorders.

A brief history of Clinical Aphasiology publications was published in 1995. Following the annual publication of the peer-reviewed manuscripts published by BRK Publishers (those manuscripts derived from those presented at the annual meeting of the CAC), the accumulation of these manuscripts has passed through a number of transitional publishers before arriving at its current publication in the *American Journal of Speech-Language Pathology (AJSLP)*, a publication of The American Speech-Language-Hearing Association (ASHA). These publishers are clearly referenced for all manuscripts. They currently reside in the hands of a diminishing number of individuals. With the opening of this archive, these valuable manuscripts will be available to the public and will record a productive history of research and scholarship stimulated in large measure by the annual meeting of the CAC.

At present, only the manuscripts derived from these publications are contained within this site. They have been entered by and at the sole expense of the University Library System (ULS), University of Pittsburgh, with the permission of the Steering Committee of the CAC and with the written permission of all previous publishers.

Administration and Support

Editorial Consultant for this project is:

Malcolm R. McNeil, PhD
Department of Communication Science and Disorders
School of Health and Rehabilitation Sciences
University of Pittsburgh

Technical support is provided by the Department of Information Systems, University Library System, University of Pittsburgh.

Contact Information

All correspondence concerning the Clinical Aphasiology archive should be sent to aphasiology@mail.pitt.edu. Please e-mail us if you have any questions or comments about the archive.

About this Software

This archive is running on eprints.org open archive software, a freely distributable archive system available from eprints.org. Other institutions are invited (and encouraged) to set up their own open archives for author self-archiving, using the freely distributable eprints.org software used at this site. This site is running software from eprints.org / revision: EPrints 2.2.1 (pepper) [Born on 2002-11-14] EPrints is free software developed by the Department of Electronics and Computer Science at the University of Southampton, England. For more information see eprints.org .

Site Administrator: aphasiology@mail.pitt.edu

The Aphasiology Archive
University Library System, University of Pittsburgh

Home ‖ About ‖ Browse ‖ Search ‖ Help

Aphasiology User Documentation

- Browsing
- Searching
  - Text Search Fields
  - Lists of Values
  - Yes/No Fields

Browsing

Browsing is a good way to access documents if you don't have a specific idea of what you're looking for. There are two ways to browse the archive, by subject and by year.

To browse the archive either select Browse from the front page or from the navigation bar at the top of the screen. Then choose which property you wish to browse by eg. "subject".

You will be presented with a list of possible values, select one of these, and you will be given a list of references to documents in the archive (if any) which match this value. To access a paper, simply click on its reference in the display.

On the abstract page, you should be able to see what subjects are pertinent to the current document. Clicking on one of those subjects will take you back to the relevant browse by subject view.

Searching

The archive offers two levels of searching, simple and advanced. They are similar, but the advanced form lets you perform a finer-grained search using more fields. Access the simple search using the Search the Archive link on the front page, or using the navigation bar at the top of the screen. To perform an advanced search, use the advanced search link at the top of the simple search page.

Text Search Fields

These are used to search fields like abstract or author. These are the fields where there is a text entry area, and a popup menu just to the right of it. Type your search terms into the box. You can decide how the system will use your search terms by selecting one of the options from the popup menu just to the right of the input box.

Match all, in any order.

In the example shown, the system will search for records in which any of the title, abstract or keywords fields contain both the word ``patient'' and ``care''.

Match any.

In the example shown, the system will search for any record with either the term ``patient'' or ``care,'' in any of the title, abstract or keywords fields.

Match as a phrase.

In this case, the system will search for your terms appearing exactly as you type them. In the example, the system will return any record with the phrase ``patient care'' appearing in the title, abstract or keywords.

Lists of Values

With these you can select one or more values from a list of values for the system to search for. If no value in the list is selected, the system will ignore this field (i.e. it will retrieve records with any value of this field.)

In cases where each individual record may have more than one value attached to the list, you can also change search behaviour by selecting ``Any of these'' or ``All of these'' from the popup menu on the right of the list.

Any of these.

> If this is selected, any record which has any of the values you select will be retrieved.

All of these.

> If you select this option, a record must have all the values you choose associated with it to be retrieved.

Years

When you're searching a year field, you can specify a single year or range of years that you're interested in:

1999
> retrieves only records where the year is `1999';

1987-1990
> retrieves records with years between 1987 and 1990 inclusive;

1995-
> retrieves records with years of 1995 or later;

-1998
> retrieves records with years up to and including 1998.

Yes/No Fields

Some fields can have the value yes or no, for example the ``Refereed'' field. In this case, the search field lets you specify whether you want retrieved records to have the value yes or no for this field, or whether you have no preference, in which case the field isn't used to find records.

Site Administrator: aphasiology@mail.pitt.edu

The Aphasiology Archive
University Library System, University of Pittsburgh

Home || About || Browse || Search || Help

Browse by Conference

Please select a value to browse from the list below.

- Conferences (1851)
  - Clinical Aphasiology Conference (1812)
    - Clinical Aphasiology Conference (1972 : 2nd : Albuquerque, NM : March 1-3, 1972) (24)
    - Clinical Aphasiology Conference (1974 : 4th : New Orleans, LA : April, 1974) (24)
    - Clinical Aphasiology Conference (1975 : 5th : Santa Fe, NM : April 30-May 2, 1975) (21)
    - Clinical Aphasiology Conference (1976 : 6th : Wemme, OR : May 18-21, 1976) (41)
    - Clinical Aphasiology Conference (1977 : 7th : Amelia Island, FL : May 17-20, 1977) (49)
    - Clinical Aphasiology Conference (1978 : 8th : Keystone, CO : May 30-June 2, 1978) (48)
    - Clinical Aphasiology Conference (1979 : 9th : Phoenix, AZ : May 28-31, 1979) (45)
    - Clinical Aphasiology Conference (1980 : 10th : Bar Harbor, ME : June 1-5, 1980) (55)
    - Clinical Aphasiology Conference (1981 : 11th : Kerrville, TX : May 10-14, 1981) (51)
    - Clinical Aphasiology Conference (1982 : 12th : Oshkosh, WI : June 6-10, 1982) (53)
    - Clinical Aphasiology Conference (1983 : 13th : Phoenix, AZ : May 29-June 2, 1983) (52)
    - Clinical Aphasiology Conference (1984 : 14th : Seabrook Island, SC : May 20-24, 1984) (47)
    - Clinical Aphasiology Conference (1985 : 15th : Ashland, OR : June 2-6, 1985) (48)
    - Clinical Aphasiology Conference (1986 : 16th : Jackson, WY : June 8-12, 1986) (50)
    - Clinical Aphasiology Conference (1987 : 17th : Lake of the Ozarks, MO : May 31-June 4, 1987) (47)
    - Clinical Aphasiology Conference (1988 : 18th : Cape Cod, MA : June 1988) (43)
    - Clinical Aphasiology Conference (1989 : 19th : Lake Tahoe, NV : June 1989) (35)
    - Clinical Aphasiology Conference (1990 : 20th : Santa Fe, NM : June 1990) (37)
    - Clinical Aphasiology Conference (1991 : 21st : Destin, FL : June 1991) (41)
    - Clinical Aphasiology Conference (1992 : 22nd : Durango, CO) (36)
    - Clinical Aphasiology Conference (1993 : 23rd : Sedona, AZ) (30)
    - Clinical Aphasiology Conference (1994 : 24th : Traverse City, MI) (28)
    - Clinical Aphasiology Conference (1995 : 25th : Sunriver, OR : June 1995) (29)
    - Clinical Aphasiology Conference (1996 : 26th : Newport, RI : June 1996) (23)
    - Clinical Aphasiology Conference (1997 : 27th : Bigfork, MO : June 1997) (26)
    - Clinical Aphasiology Conference (1998 : 28th : Asheville, NC : June 1998) (22)
    - Clinical Aphasiology Conference (1999 : 29th : Key West, FL : June 1999) (19)
    - Clinical Aphasiology Conference (2000 : 30th : Waikoloa Beach, HI : May 2000) (20)
    - Clinical Aphasiology Conference (2001 : 31st : Santa Fe, NM : May 29-June 2, 2001) (24)
    - Clinical Aphasiology Conference (2002 : 32nd : Ridgedale, MO : June 2002) (12)
    - Clinical Aphasiology Conference (2003 : 33rd : Orcas Island, WA : May 2003) (19)
    - Clinical Aphasiology Conference (2004 : 34th : Park City, UT : May 2004) (70)
    - Clinical Aphasiology Conference (2005 : 35th : Sanibel Island, FL : May 31-June 4, 2005) (52)
    - Clinical Aphasiology Conference (2006 : 36th : Ghent, Belgium : May 29-June 2, 2006) (83)
    - Clinical Aphasiology Conference (2007 : 37th : Scottsdale, AZ : May 22-26, 2007) (76)
    - Clinical Aphasiology Conference (2008 : 38th : Jackson Hole, WY : May 27 - June 1, 2008) (73)
    - Clinical Aphasiology Conference (2009 : 39th : Keystone, CO : May 26-30, 2009) (89)
    - Clinical Aphasiology Conference (2010 : 40th : Isle of Palms, SC : May 23-27, 2010) (89)
    - Clinical Aphasiology Conference (2011 : 41st : Fort Lauderdale, FL : May 31-June 4, 2011) (96)
    - Clinical Aphasiology Conference (2012 : 42nd : Lake Tahoe, CA : May 20-25, 2012) (81)
    - Clinical Aphasiology Conference (2013 : 43rd : Tucson, AZ : May 28-June 2, 2013) (79)
  - International Aphasia Rehabilitation Conference (39)
    - International Aphasia Rehabilitation Conference (2006: 12th: Sheffield, U.K.: 4-6 June, 2006) (39)

Site Administrator: aphasiology@mail.pitt.edu

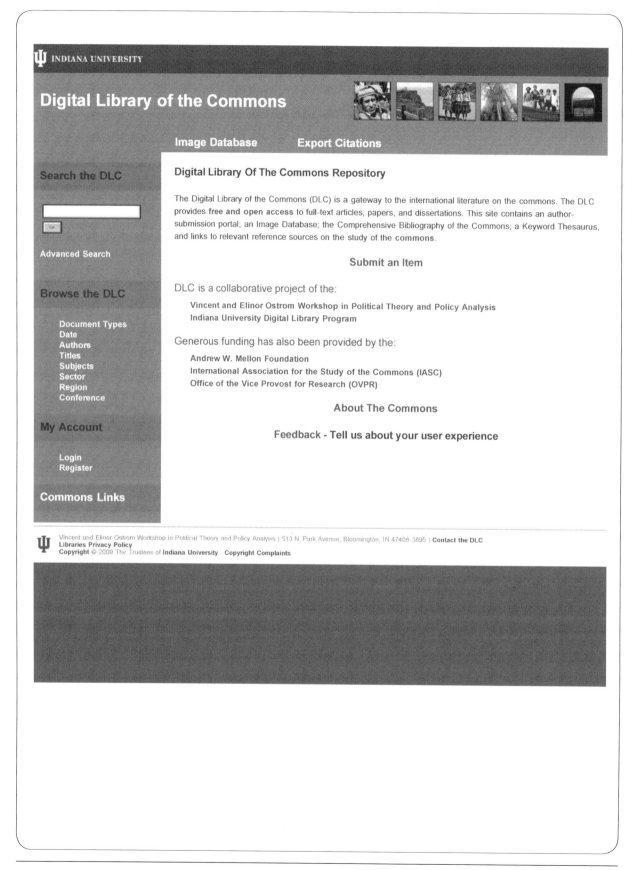

INDIANA UNIVERSITY

Digital Library of the Commons

Image Database   Export Citations

Search the DLC

[   ]

[Go]

Advanced Search

Browse the DLC

> Document Types
> Date
> Authors
> Titles
> Subjects
> Sector
> Region
> Conference

My Account

> Login
> Register

Commons Links

Digital Library Of The Commons Repository

The Digital Library of the Commons (DLC) is a gateway to the international literature on the commons. The DLC provides free and open access to full-text articles, papers, and dissertations. This site contains an author-submission portal; an Image Database; the Comprehensive Bibliography of the Commons; a Keyword Thesaurus, and links to relevant reference sources on the study of the commons.

Submit an Item

DLC is a collaborative project of the:

> Vincent and Elinor Ostrom Workshop in Political Theory and Policy Analysis
> Indiana University Digital Library Program

Generous funding has also been provided by the:

Andrew W. Mellon Foundation
International Association for the Study of the Commons (IASC)
Office of the Vice Provost for Research (OVPR)

About The Commons

Feedback - Tell us about your user experience

Agriculture

Includes: agrarian reform; agricultural expansion; agroecology; agroforestry; agrotechnology; alley farming; cash cropping; communal or group farming; cropping systems; desertification; drought and erosion management; dryland management; ejidos; family farming; farm forestry; farm policy; farmers' associations; gardening; history of agricultural management; household food production; indigenous agriculture; participatory rural appraisal (PRA); rapid rural appraisal (RRA); rural development; shifting cultivation; soil conservation; swidden fallows; terracing; etc.

Also, names of individual crops: cocoa, cotton, rice, etc.

(See also Forestry, Land Tenure and Use, and Water Resources Sectors)

Fisheries

Includes: aquaculture; artisanal fisheries; co-management; coral reefs; fisheries' history; ITQs; limited entry; mariculture; marine property rights; quotas; sealing; seine fishing, shellfisheries; stewardship, whaling etc.

Also, types of fish: cod, crab, salmon, etc.

Also, types of fishing vessels and fishing technologies

(See also Water Resources and Global Commons Sectors)

Forest Resources

Includes: afforestation; agroforestry; buffer zones; certification clearcutting; community forestry; deforestation; ejidos; forest management; forest policy; forest products; fuelwood; harvesting, hunters and gatherers; plantations; rainforests; sacred groves; savannahs; silviculture; soil conservation; stewardship, timber; tropical forests; woodlots, etc.

Also: names of trees and forest products: acacia, bamboo, mangrove, palm, etc.

Also: research technology and methods, such as GIS, mapping, remote sensing, etc.

(See also Agriculture, Grazing, Land Tenure and Use, Water Resources, Wildlife Sectors)

General and Multiple-use Commons

Includes: biodiversity; conservation; ecology; ecosystems, environmental management; environmental policy; multiple resource management; multiple-use; natural resources; pollution; resource sharing; rural development; sustainable development, etc.

(See also: Global Commons Sector)

Global Commons

Includes: acid rain, air pollution, air slots, atmosphere, carbon sequestration; climate change, electro-magnetic spectrum, governance and management of arctic regions; global warming, greenhouse effect; international treaties; oceans, outer space; governance, law and management of transboundary resources; transboundary disputes, radio spectrum, etc.

Grazing Areas

Includes: cattle grazing; herding systems; husbandry; livestock management; nomads; overgrazing; pastoralism; range management; rangelands, transhumance, etc. Also: reindeer, caribou,etc.

(See also Agriculture, Land Tenure and Use, Forestry, and Wildlife Sectors)

History

Includes historical publications

ex.: Cook, G. W. [1856] *The Acts for Facilitating the Inclosure of Commons in England and Wales...*

Also includes modern publications about the history of common pool and common property resources

ex.: Norberg, K. [1988] "Dividing up the Commons: Institutional Change in Rural France, 1789-1799." *Politics and Society* 16:265-286.

Information and Knowledge Commons

Includes: anticommons, copyright, indigenous, local, scientific knowledge issues, intellectual property rights, the Internet, libraries, patents, virtual commons, etc.

(See also Nontraditional CPRs and Social Organization Sectors)

Land Tenure and Use

Includes: arid regions; boundaries; communal lands; customary land law; enclosure; land degradation; land economics; landowners; property rights; public lands; smallholder, etc.

(See also Agriculture, Grazing, Forestry)

New Commons (also called Nontraditional CPRs)

Examples: air slots, budgets, cable TV, campus commons, radio spectrum, tourism management, roads, etc.

(See also Information and Knowledge Commons and Urban Commons)

Social Organization

Includes: capacity building; clans; class structure; collectives; community organization and participation; cultural history; ejidos; ethnicity; family structure; gender; governance systems; group behavior; households; indigenous institutions; institutional change; kibbutzim; kinship; panchayats; participatory management; peasants; sherpas; social change; social conflict; social norms; tribal structure, village organization; women, etc.

(See also Information and Knowledge, Theory and General & Multiple-Use Sectors)

Theory & Experimental

Includes: adaptive systems; agent-based computational economics; club goods; collective action; common property regimes and rights; complexity; conflict resolution; cooperation; covenantal theory; decision making; design principles; economics, institutional, and legal history; ecological economics; efficiency; experimental economics; free riding; game theory; IAD framework; institutional analysis; institutional economics; mechanism design; models; new institutionalism; norms; policy, prisoner's dilemma' property rights; public goods and bads; reciprocity; rent seeking; rules; scarcity; self-governance; simulations; social capital; tragedy of the commons; trust, etc.

(Also search above keywords in combination with all other Sectors).

Urban Commons

Includes: apartment complexes and housing collectives; city commons; industrialized areas; parking, playgrounds, sidewalks, waste management, urban greenspace, urban forestry, etc.

(See also New Commons Sector).

Water Resources

Includes: canals; coastal management; coral reefs; dams; dyke management; groundwater, huertas; irrigation systems; marine policy; river management; riparian rights; sea tenure; watersheds; water pollution; water scarcity, etc.

(See also Fisheries, Agriculture, & Forestry Sectors).

Wildlife

Examples: animal conservation and protection; biological diversity; CAMPFIRE (Zimbabwean project); endangered species; hunters and gatherers; indigenous management systems; poaching; etc.

(See also Fisheries Sector for aquatic animals; and Grazing for livestock, cattle and rangeland management).

Dryad

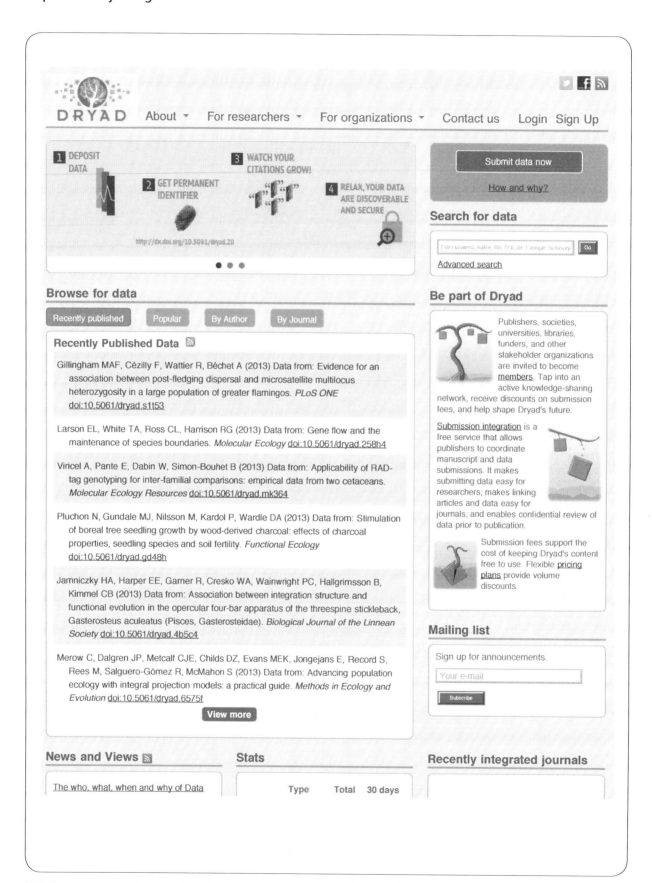

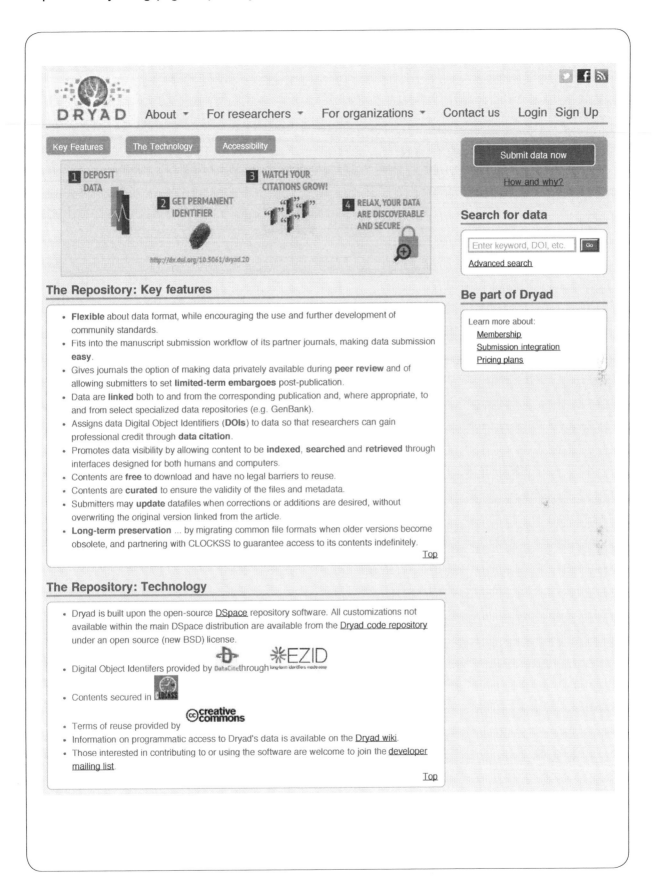

Accessibility Statement

Overview:

Dryad's mission is to make the data underlying scholarly publications **discoverable**, **accessible**, **understandable**, **freely reusable**, and **citable** for all users. We believe that universal design and adherence to coding standards are the best means to ensure access to the broadest possible audience, and our design and development staff work together to achieve those goals.

Section 508 Compliance:

To ensure that we meet or exceed the requirements of the 1998 Amendment to Section 508 of the Rehabilitation Act of 1973, Dryad continually reviews our site and modifies pages to remove accessibility problems for people with disabilities. Our website uses HTML that follows Section 508 standards; for example, we include alternate text to describe graphics. We use accessibility testing tools to help us find and fix issues whenever we add new features of content. For more detailed information on the 508 compliance status of the Dryad website, please see our Voluntary Product Accessibility Template® (Dryad-VPAT.PDF 🖂).

Accessibility of Dryad Contents

The Dryad Repository does not impose any file format restrictions. As a result, Dryad cannot guarantee that all files in all data packages are accessible. However, we encourage authors to submit data in formats such as ASCII and HTML that are not only accessible to screen reading software, but also more suitable for preservation and reuse.

What to do if you have a problem

If you have a problem accessing any page on the Dryad website, please contact help@datadryad.org and we will work to resolve the problem.

Top

Last revised: 2013-11-01

Dryad is a nonprofit repository for data underlying the international scientific and medical literature.

Terms of Service | Contact Us

Powered by D SPACE

Latest build Mon, 25 Nov 2013 16:42:33 EST. Served by North Carolina State University

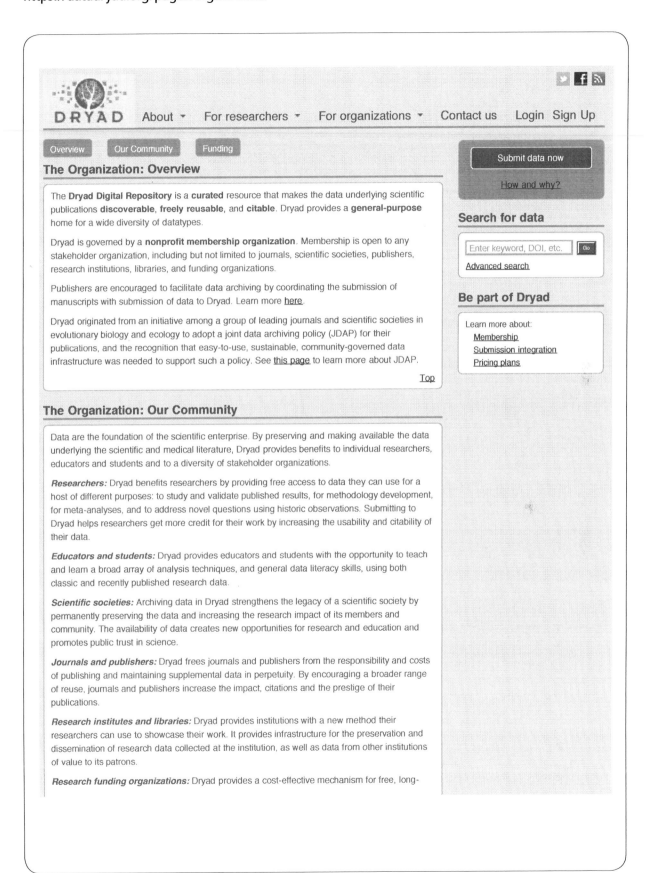

The Organization: Overview

The **Dryad Digital Repository** is a **curated** resource that makes the data underlying scientific publications **discoverable**, **freely reusable**, and **citable**. Dryad provides a **general-purpose** home for a wide diversity of datatypes.

Dryad is governed by a **nonprofit membership organization**. Membership is open to any stakeholder organization, including but not limited to journals, scientific societies, publishers, research institutions, libraries, and funding organizations.

Publishers are encouraged to facilitate data archiving by coordinating the submission of manuscripts with submission of data to Dryad. Learn more here.

Dryad originated from an initiative among a group of leading journals and scientific societies in evolutionary biology and ecology to adopt a joint data archiving policy (JDAP) for their publications, and the recognition that easy-to-use, sustainable, community-governed data infrastructure was needed to support such a policy. See this page to learn more about JDAP.

Top

The Organization: Our Community

Data are the foundation of the scientific enterprise. By preserving and making available the data underlying the scientific and medical literature, Dryad provides benefits to individual researchers, educators and students and to a diversity of stakeholder organizations.

Researchers: Dryad benefits researchers by providing free access to data they can use for a host of different purposes: to study and validate published results, for methodology development, for meta-analyses, and to address novel questions using historic observations. Submitting to Dryad helps researchers get more credit for their work by increasing the usability and citability of their data.

Educators and students: Dryad provides educators and students with the opportunity to teach and learn a broad array of analysis techniques, and general data literacy skills, using both classic and recently published research data.

Scientific societies: Archiving data in Dryad strengthens the legacy of a scientific society by permanently preserving the data and increasing the research impact of its members and community. The availability of data creates new opportunities for research and education and promotes public trust in science.

Journals and publishers: Dryad frees journals and publishers from the responsibility and costs of publishing and maintaining supplemental data in perpetuity. By encouraging a broader range of reuse, journals and publishers increase the impact, citations and the prestige of their publications.

Research institutes and libraries: Dryad provides institutions with a new method their researchers can use to showcase their work. It provides infrastructure for the preservation and dissemination of research data collected at the institution, as well as data from other institutions of value to its patrons.

Research funding organizations: Dryad provides a cost-effective mechanism for free, long-

Submit data now

How and why?

Search for data

Enter keyword, DOI, etc.   Go

Advanced search

Be part of Dryad

Learn more about:
Membership
Submission integration
Pricing plans

term access to data which, in turn, enables new research. Data availability improves the rigor of the scientific record and public trust in the scientific enterprise.

Top

The Organization: Funding

Dryad gratefully acknowledges support from the following organizations. Any opinions, findings, and conclusions or recommendations expressed in this material are those of the project staff and do not necessarily reflect the views of the funders.

Current awards

- "Scalable and sustainable infrastructure for the publication of data", from the U.S. National Science Foundation, 2012-2016.
- "DataNetONE (Observation Network for Earth)", from the U.S. National Science Foundation, 2009-2014.
- Support from The National Evolutionary Synthesis Center through a cooperative agreement with the U.S. National Science Foundation (DBI-0905606), 2007-2014.

Past awards

- "A Digital Repository for Preservation and Sharing of Data Underlying Published Works in Evolutionary Biology", U.S. National Science Foundation, 2008-2012.
- "Helping Interdisciplinary Vocabulary Engineering", from the U.S. Institute for Museum and Library Services, 2009-2012.
- "The DryadUK project", from the JISC in the UK, 2010-2011.

Top

Last revised: 2013-04-11

Dryad is a nonprofit repository for data underlying the international scientific and medical literature.

Terms of Service | Contact Us

Powered by ▢▨▢ D SPACE

Latest build Mon, 25 Nov 2013 16:42:33 EST. Served by North Carolina State University

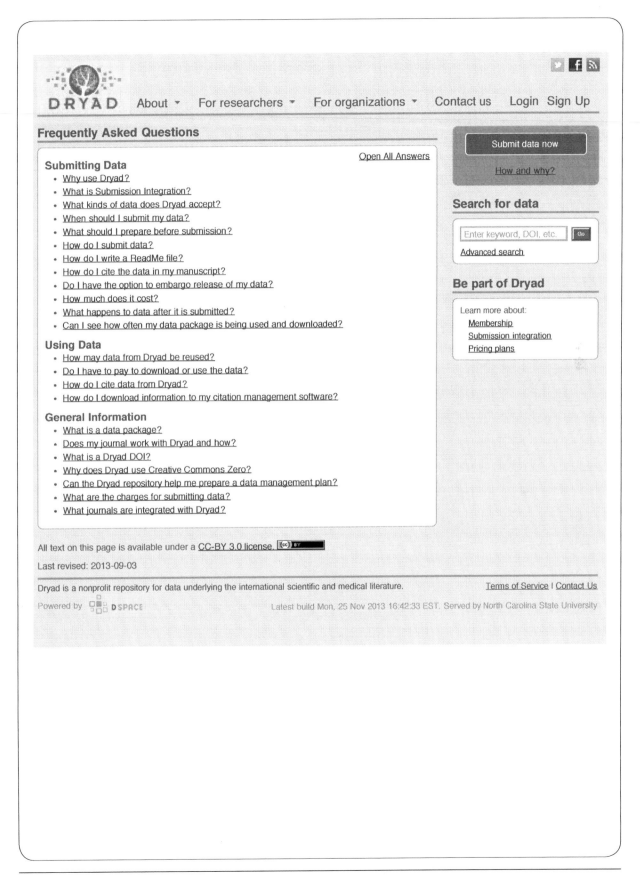

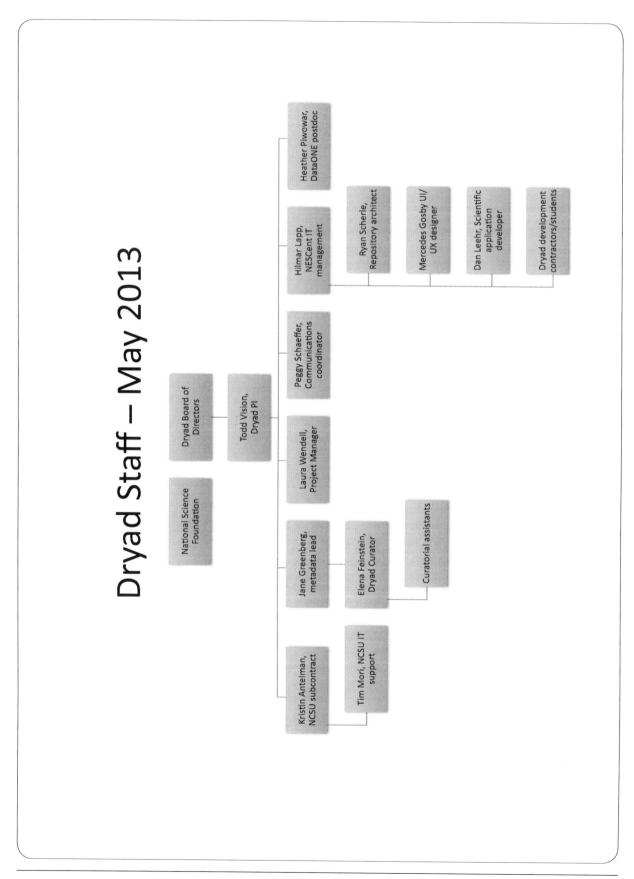

PhilSci-Archive

PHILSCI-ARCHIVE
An Archive for Preprints in Philosophy of Science
http://philsci-archive.pitt.edu/

Login | Create Account

Search & Browse

Simple Search

Advanced Search

Browse by Subject

Browse by Year

Browse by Conferences/Volumes

Latest Additions

Information

Home

About the Archive

Archive Policy

History

Help

FAQ

Journal Eprint Policies

Register

Contact Us

News

Guide to new PhilSci-Archive features.

PhilSci-Archive Poster

An Archive for Preprints in Philosophy of Science

Welcome to PhilSci-Archive, an electronic archive for **preprints** in the philosophy of science. It is offered as a free service to the philosophy of science community. The goal of the archive is to promote communication in the field by the rapid dissemination of new work. PhilSci-Archive invites submissions in all areas of philosophy of science, including general philosophy of science, philosophy of particular sciences (physics, biology, chemistry, psychology, etc.), feminist philosophy of science, socially relevant philosophy of science, history and philosophy of science and history of the philosophy of science.

| Enter Title, Keywords, or Author | Search |

Help / FAQ
Simple / Advanced Search

Viewing Material on PhilSci-Archive

There are several ways to view material in the archive. Do a simple search using the box above, or do an **Advanced Search** to find something specific. You can also simply browse PhilSci-Archive for particular subjects, years and conferences using the links in the sidebar to the left.

You can receive alerts when new posts appear on PhilSci-Archive, either by email, or by your favorite RSS reader. Signing up is easy: just choose one of PhilSci-Archive's various **Notification Options**.

Posting Material on PhilSci-Archive

First time posters should first consult the **Archive Policy**, and then **create a new account**. Once logged in, click the "New Item" button to start the process of uploading your paper to PhilSci-Archive.

By posting a preprint on PhilSci-Archive, you can share your work with thousands of subscribing philosophers of science. Posts can be updated with new versions or links to the publication when it appears in a journal. The posting of preprints is also encouraged by most philosophy of science journals. For individual journal policies, please consult this **list**.

Conference and Volume Sections

There is a special section for those organizing conferences or preparing volumes of papers and seeking an easy way to circulate advance copies of papers. Invited participants can **follow these instructions** to post their papers on a designated conference or volume page. This page can now also be used to automatically generate a PDF preprint volume upon request. **More about PDF preprint volumes...**

If you would like to add your conference or volume, or create a PDF preprint volume, contact PhilSci-Archive at **philsci-archive@mail.pitt.edu.**

Sponsored by

- Philosophy of Science Association
- Center for Philosophy of Science, University of Pittsburgh
- University Library System, University of Pittsburgh

Statistics

- There are currently **3448** articles available in this archive.

PhilSci-Archive supports **OAI 2.0** with a base URL of http://philsci-archive.pitt.edu/cgi/oai2

| ULS D-Scribe | E-Prints | Share | Get Alerts for All New Posts |

Get daily alerts via:

Login | Create Account

Search & Browse

Simple Search
Advanced Search
Browse by Subject
Browse by Year
Browse by Conferences/Volumes
Latest Additions

Information

Home
About the Archive
Archive Policy
History
Help
FAQ
Journal Eprint Policies
Register
Contact Us

News

Guide to new PhilSci-Archive features.
PhilSci-Archive Poster

About the Archive

Administration and Support

Archive Board

Jeffrey A. Barrett (Editor-in-Chief, Philosophy of Science, ex officio)
William Bechtel
Zvi Biener
John Earman
Michela Massimi
Roberta Millstein (Governing Board, Philosophy of Science Association, ex officio)
John D. Norton
Bryan W. Roberts
Justin Sytsma
C. Kenneth Waters

Officers of the Board

Coordinator: John D. Norton
Alternate Coordinator: John Earman
Conferences and Volumes: Bryan Roberts
Editorial Chair: Zvi Biener and Michela Massimi
Promotions and Outreach: Bill Bechtel and Roberta Millstein
Website Quality: Justin Sytsma

Archive Manager

Thomas Pashby

PhilSci-Archive Consultant

Michael Miller

Constitution of the Archive Board

1. The Board is comprised of philosophers of science with recognized standing in the profession.

2. The number of members on the Board is determined by the need to:

   o provide sufficient members for the Officer positions listed above and to discharge other Board duties, including the moderation of submissions to the archive.
   o provide good representation of the profession.

3. Board members are appointed for three year, renewable terms. Membership of the Board and extension of membership term is by invitation from a consensus of current Board members.

4. Two Board members are:

   o a member of the Governing Board of the Philosophy of Science Association, appointed ex officio.
   o the editor-in-chief or an associate editor of the journal Philosophy of Science, appointed ex officio.

Duties of Officers and Staff

Coordinator: Responsible for the good functioning and coordination of all archive activities.

Alternate Coordinator: Serves as Coordinator when the primary Coordinator is unavailable.

Conferences and Volumes: Responsible for the soliciting and maintenance of the conferences and volumes section and the preparation of combined volumes as PDF files.

Editorial Chair: Chairs the discussion concerning moderation of submissions to the archive.

Promotions and Outreach: Responsible for maintaining visibility of the archive and encouraging wider usage in the philosophy of science profession.

Website Quality: Responsible for oversight of the academic and editorial content of the PhilSci-Archive and the user experience.

Archive Manager: Responsible for daily editorial activities, including initial phases of moderation, responding to user queries, keeping records of posting activities and implementing routine maintenance. The manager holds the only remunerated position.

PhilSci-Archive Consultant: Provides technical assistance to the Archive Manager.

Contact Information

Any correspondence concerning this specific archive should be sent to philsci-archive@mail.pitt.edu.

System Information

This site is powered by EPrints 3, free software developed by the University of Southampton.

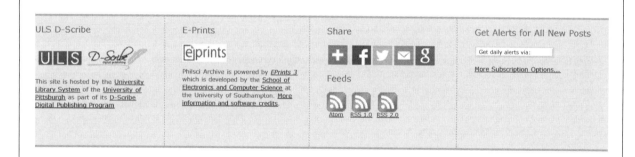

ULS D-Scribe

This site is hosted by the University Library System of the University of Pittsburgh as part of its D-Scribe Digital Publishing Program

E-Prints

Philsci Archive is powered by EPrints 3 which is developed by the School of Electronics and Computer Science at the University of Southampton. More information and software credits.

Share

Feeds

Atom   RSS 1.0   RSS 2.0

Get Alerts for All New Posts

Get daily alerts via:

More Subscription Options...

Login | Create Account

Search & Browse

Simple Search

Advanced Search

Browse by Subject

Browse by Year

Browse by
Conferences/Volumes

Latest Additions

Information

Home

About the Archive

Archive Policy

History

Help

FAQ

Journal Eprint Policies

Register

Contact Us

News

Guide to new PhilSci-
Archive features.

PhilSci-Archive Poster

Archive Policy

Submissions

PhilSci-Archive is offered by its sponsors as a free service to philosophers of science. Its goal is to preserve and foster the rapid exchange of new work in philosophy of science

Preprints posted on the archive are restricted to those in philosophy of science or related material of interest to professional philosophers of science. The range of admissible topics and the style of analysis is set by the topics and styles of material publishable in the Philosophy of Science Association journal, *Philosophy of Science.*

The archive posts complete, self-contained papers that have achieved a stable form. It strongly discourages repeated postings to correct errors in papers posted in haste. The archive does not post short notes, letters and other material that do not fit the model of a scholarly paper. The archive does not support threaded discussions.

The archive also posts separate "publication" records, whose use is restricted to informing archive users of the published article derived from a preprint already posted on the archive. These records include a link to the journal publication deriving from a preprint on the archive and do not require the uploading of a document.

Since the content of the archive is moderated, we regret that we can only accept papers written in English. This applies to general submissions only; conference organizers may formulate their own language policies for conference sections. (rule revised May 15, 2009)

Up to two business days should be allowed between the time a paper is deposited to the archive and the time it becomes accessible to other users of the archive.

Rejections

The archive reserves the right to refuse to post papers it deems to lie outside these boundaries. Because of the volume of material posted, the archive cannot enter into correspondence concerning submissions that have been refused.

Disclaimer

No representation is made by the archive on the accuracy or quality of preprints posted. The views and opinions expressed are those of the authors and not the archive sponsors. With respect to the documents available from this server, the archive sponsors make no warranty, expressed or implied, including warrants of merchantability, fitness for a particular purpose and non-infringement, and the sponsors do not assume any liability or responsibility for the accuracy, completeness, or usefulness of any information or material.

All documents available from this server may be protected under U.S. and foreign copyright laws, and may not be reproduced without permission.

The archive takes the act of posting a paper as a representation by the person posting that the paper does not contain libelous or defamatory material, that the person posting the paper owns the copyright to it and grants users of the archive permission to make a copy of the paper for their private use.

Removals

PhilSci-Archive will honor all requests from authors for the removal of files they deposited along with their associated bibliographic metadata. See the (FAQ dealing with removal.) However, note that most journals do *not* require the removal of a preprint upon publication. Authors can check a journal's copyright policy by visiting Sherpa/Romeo.

Out of Print

PhilSci-Archive accepts a small number of out of print texts in philosophy of science, strictly limited to texts that, in the judgment of PhilSci Archive, are of central importance in philosophy of science and are still sought by present-day philosophers of science. Proposals for such texts should be made informally by email to philsci-archive@mail.pitt.edu.

Before any works proposed can be posted, they must be free of copyright encumbrance. That may be the case already if the text is sufficiently old to be in the public domain, as are works published under US copyright prior to 1923. However, copyright law is complicated and it may not always be clear if a text is in the public domain. See http:// www.copyright.gov/. For works for which a copyright is still in force, written permission to reproduce the work online must be obtained from the copyright holder. Since we expect to post a limited number of volumes only, we ask that proposers contact philsci-archive to discuss the proposed volume, before any approach to a copyright holder is made.

Login | Create Account |

Resources in Integrated Care
FOR MORBIDITY MANAGEMENT AND DISABILITY PREVENTION

Information

Home

News *(Coming soon)*

About RIIC-4MMDP

Policies

Help

Search and Browse

Search

Search

Advanced Search

Browse

Latest Additions

Welcome to Resources in Integrated Care (RIIC) for Morbidity Management and Disability Prevention (4MMDP)

RIIC-4MMDP is a free, open access, online "self-archiving" repository dedicated to sharing best practices, lessons learned, and exploring new strategies for MMDP with the wider MMDP community. The primary goal is to aid countries as they build capacity for planning, implementing, monitoring and evaluating MMDP activities. As acknowledged by others in the fight against disabling diseases, the most important tool for achieving goals in disease control efforts is *knowledge; promoting its enhancement, sharing and utilization* (Koporc 2013). Disease control efforts are enhanced when integrated with MMDP activities (Cantey, Rout et al. 2010).

To achieve its goal, RIIC-4MMDP hopes to centralize all MMDP content with a custom interface that makes it easy to find what you need and to navigate through it (every word in each document is searchable). In addition to published research, content includes contributions developed by National Ministries of Health and Education and practical field materials produced by NGOs and their technical consultants, materials that are not easily accessible and searchable by other means.

Cantey, P., J. Rout, et al. (2010). "Increasing compliance with mass drug administration programs for lymphatic filariasis in India through education and lymphedema management programs." PLoS Negl Trop Dis 4(6): e728.

Koporc, K. (2013). Building on Strong Foundations: CWWäs First Eight Years, and the Way Forward. Quarterly Dose, Children Without Worms: Partnership for Treating and Preventing Intestinal Worms.

Features

- Centralized MMDP resources eliminating the need to search for MMDP materials across disease-specific websites
- Centralized important but hard-to-find and little published "grey" literature
- Enhanced discoverability and visibility of content: refereed and non-refereed articles, guidelines, reports, news, events notices, conference/workshop proceedings, published and unpublished materials, and multimedia (graphics, PowerPoint, video, audio, etc.)
- Permanent preservation of content
- Rapid dissemination through social networking tools like Facebook/Twitter, RSS feeds, email alerts
- Links to existing websites whenever possible
- Evidence-based support and ongoing research for decision-making by program managers, health workers, and scholars alike
- Free, direct contributions to the repository by the MMDP community for both peer-reviewed and non-peer-reviewed materials*

* Content experts are used for editorial review, control, and to assure quality, relevance, and usability.

Definitions

RIIC-4MMDP defines "integrated care" as *patient-centered, community-based health interventions focused on crosscutting issues common to many disabling diseases/chronic conditions.* Integrated care is cost-effective, prevents duplication of services, provides a more uniform approach to early detection and care, and builds synergy among health care workers and within health care systems.

Integrated care promotes:

- Patient-centered care and self-care for chronic conditions
- Integration of MMDP with disease control interventions
- Training affected persons and their families, community volunteers and health workers concurrently to act as a team
- Sustainable interventions and technologies
- Capacity building across the continuum of care

RIIC-4MMDP is the official publisher of materials developed by the **Integrated Care for Morbidity Management and Disability Prevention Initiative** (www.icare4mmdp.org). Contributors of MMDP materials include governments, nongovernmental organizations, multilateral organizations and initiatives, professional organizations, academic and research institutions, and individuals.

Contents

Materials submitted must deal with some crosscutting aspect of community-based morbidity management and disability prevention (as defined above). Contributions to the resource center must not only be relevant to at least one of the six (6) main themes below, but must also be applicable to less-resourced environments (link to subject tree).

Subject Categories

- Effective community actions to prevent disabling diseases/conditions

  Examples:

    - clean water
    - proper sanitation
    - education for healthy living

- Early detection of diseases and harmful conditions in the community

  Examples:

    - identification of affected persons
    - identification of disability
    - when/where to refer, etc.

- Community-based treatment, restoration of function, and ongoing care

  Examples:

    - eye care
    - skin and nail care
    - wound care and scar care
    - edema management
    - exercise
    - assistive technology, footwear, etc.

- Community actions to improve or eliminate activity limitations and/or participation restrictions

  Examples:

- self-care groups
- community-based rehabilitation
- prevention of disability committees
- stigma reduction activities, etc.

- Supportive strategies to strengthen community engagement and improve the sustainability of community-based care

Examples:

- vocational or occupational training
- leadership training for youth
- community development programs, etc.
- empowerment activities, etc.

- Capacity building across the continuum of care

Examples:

- MMDP curricula
- training for health care workers at the referral level
- information and communication technology (mHealth), etc.

Role of the Editorial Team

The RIIC-4MMDP editorial team is made up of either individual content experts and/or individuals that provide a conduit for content experts from one or more of the fields in the defined subject areas. These larger groups are generally comprised of disease-specific or intervention-specific organizations. Thus, the editorial team is made up of committed individuals who contribute significantly to the repository in terms of the volume and the quality of material and/or ensure such contributions for a larger group of stakeholders. In achieving this goal, editorial team members commit to providing staff/students to deposit materials and supervise the process.

Because the editorial team is largely responsible for the content of the RIIC-4MMDP, members are responsible not only for contributions from defined subject areas but encourage contributions from the MMDP community at large. Therefore, the editorial team promotes RIIC-4MMDP at meetings, conferences, and symposia, in related journals and through interactions with the wider MMDP community. The editorial team provides leadership in the use of the repository as a resource for countries and provides feedback on the usability of the repository for continuous quality improvement.

It is not within the scope of editorial team members to evaluate the quality or scientific merit of a creative work. Editorial team members, or the content experts they represent, review and control deposited material to assure quality, relevance, and usability of the materials. They review to assure that:

- Submitted material has been correctly coded for submission (e.g. type of work, published vs. unpublished, etc.)
- Permission has been obtained (if required)
- Submitted materials meet the content specifications in terms of relevance and usability

Editorial Team (TBD)

Represent the following disease/condition-specific groups (TBD)

- Buruli Ulcer
- Chagas
- Cysticerosis
- Dengue
- Diabetes
- FB Trematode
- Guinea worm
- H Afro Trypanosomiasis
- HIV/AIDS

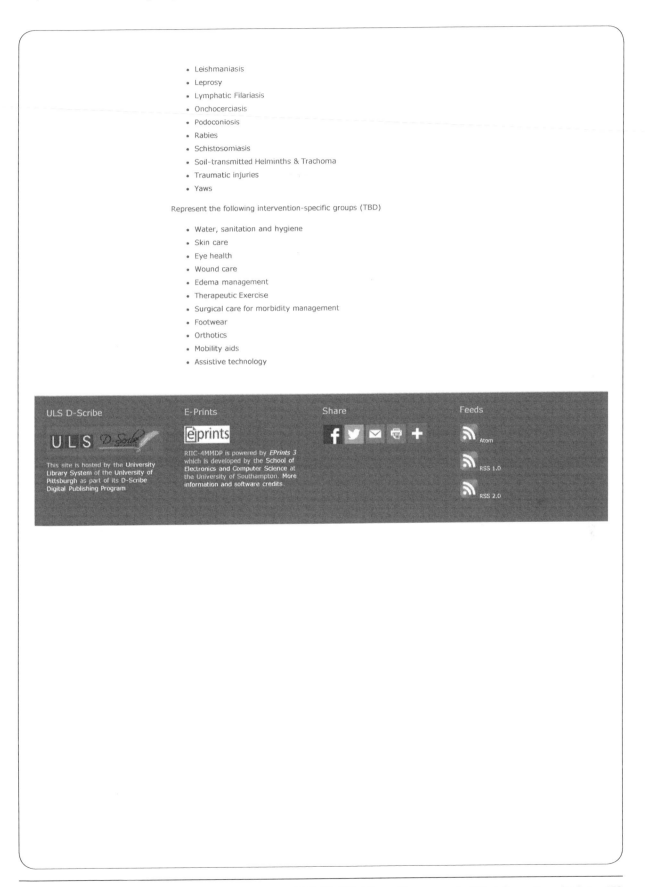

- Leishmaniasis
- Leprosy
- Lymphatic Filariasis
- Onchocerciasis
- Podoconiosis
- Rabies
- Schistosomiasis
- Soil-transmitted Helminths & Trachoma
- Traumatic injuries
- Yaws

Represent the following intervention-specific groups (TBD)

- Water, sanitation and hygiene
- Skin care
- Eye health
- Wound care
- Edema management
- Therapeutic Exercise
- Surgical care for morbidity management
- Footwear
- Orthotics
- Mobility aids
- Assistive technology

ULS D-Scribe

This site is hosted by the University Library System of the University of Pittsburgh as part of its D-Scribe Digital Publishing Program

E-Prints

RIIC-4MMDP is powered by EPrints 3 which is developed by the School of Electronics and Computer Science at the University of Southampton. More information and software credits.

Share

Feeds

Atom

RSS 1.0

RSS 2.0

4. Items may not normally be removed from RIIC-4MMDP.

5. Acceptable reasons for withdrawal include:

   - Proven copyright violation or plagiarism
   - Legal requirements and proven violations
   - National Security
   - Falsified research

6. Withdrawn items are not deleted *per se*, but are removed from public view.

7. Withdrawn items' identifiers/URLs are retained indefinitely.

8. URLs will continue to point to 'tombstone' citations, to avoid broken links and to retain item histories.

9. *Errata* and *corrigenda* lists may be included with the original record if required.

10. If necessary, an updated version may be deposited.

11. No closure policy defined.

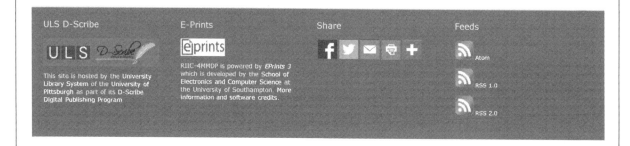

ULS D-Scribe

This site is hosted by the University Library System of the University of Pittsburgh as part of its D-Scribe Digital Publishing Program

E-Prints

RIIC-4MMDP is powered by *EPrints 3* which is developed by the School of Electronics and Computer Science at the University of Southampton. More information and software credits.

Share

Feeds

Atom

RSS 1.0

RSS 2.0

Archive of European Integration

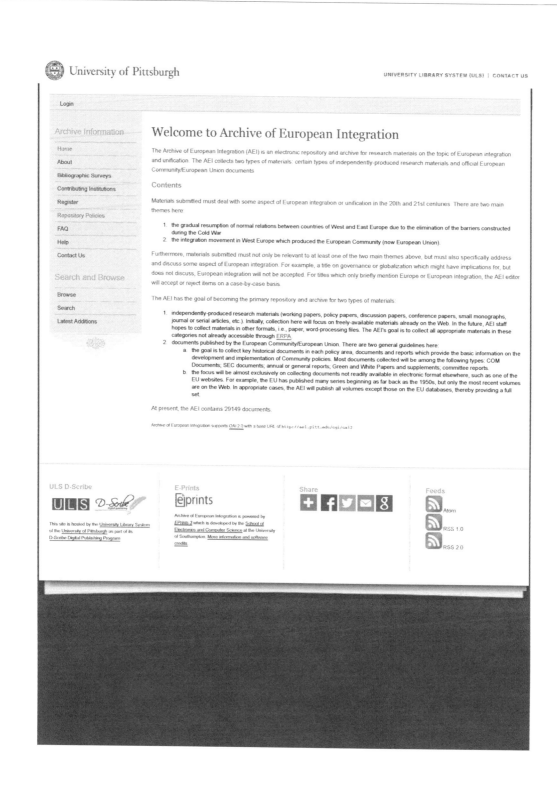

University of Pittsburgh

UNIVERSITY LIBRARY SYSTEM (ULS) | CONTACT US

Login

Archive Information

Home
About
Bibliographic Surveys
Contributing Institutions
Register
Repository Policies
FAQ
Help
Contact Us

Search and Browse

Browse
Search
Latest Additions

Welcome to Archive of European Integration

The Archive of European Integration (AEI) is an electronic repository and archive for research materials on the topic of European integration and unification. The AEI collects two types of materials: certain types of independently-produced research materials and official European Community/European Union documents

Contents

Materials submitted must deal with some aspect of European integration or unification in the 20th and 21st centuries. There are two main themes here:

1. the gradual resumption of normal relations between countries of West and East Europe due to the elimination of the barriers constructed during the Cold War
2. the integration movement in West Europe which produced the European Community (now European Union).

Furthermore, materials submitted must not only be relevant to at least one of the two main themes above, but must also specifically address and discuss some aspect of European integration. For example, a title on governance or globalization which might have implications for, but does not discuss, European integration will not be accepted. For titles which only briefly mention Europe or European integration, the AEI editor will accept or reject items on a case-by-case basis.

The AEI has the goal of becoming the primary repository and archive for two types of materials:

1. independently-produced research materials (working papers, policy papers, discussion papers, conference papers, small monographs, journal or serial articles, etc.). Initially, collection here will focus on freely-available materials already on the Web. In the future, AEI staff hopes to collect materials in other formats, i.e., paper, word-processing files. The AEI's goal is to collect all appropriate materials in these categories not already accessible through ERPA.
2. documents published by the European Community/European Union. There are two general guidelines here:
   a. the goal is to collect key historical documents in each policy area, documents and reports which provide the basic information on the development and implementation of Community policies. Most documents collected will be among the following types: COM Documents; SEC documents; annual or general reports; Green and White Papers and supplements; committee reports.
   b. the focus will be almost exclusively on collecting documents not readily available in electronic format elsewhere, such as one of the EU websites. For example, the EU has published many series beginning as far back as the 1950s, but only the most recent volumes are on the Web. In appropriate cases, the AEI will publish all volumes except those on the EU databases, thereby providing a full set.

At present, the AEI contains 29149 documents.

Archive of European Integration supports OAI 2.0 with a base URL of http://aei.pitt.edu/cgi/oai2

ULS D-Scribe

ULS D-Scribe

This site is hosted by the University Library System of the University of Pittsburgh as part of its D-Scribe Digital Publishing Program

E-Prints

eprints

Archive of European Integration is powered by EPrints 3 which is developed by the School of Electronics and Computer Science at the University of Southampton. More information and software credits

Share

Feeds

Atom
RSS 1.0
RSS 2.0

University of Pittsburgh

UNIVERSITY LIBRARY SYSTEM (ULS) | CONTACT US

Login

Archive Information

Home

About

Bibliographic Surveys

Contributing Institutions

Register

Repository Policies

FAQ

Help

Contact Us

Search and Browse

Browse

Search

Latest Additions

About the Archive

Contact Information

Any correspondence concerning this specific archive should be sent to aei@mail.pitt.edu

Archive Policy

- Archive Policy

AEI Privacy Policy

- AEI Privacy Policy

History

The Archive of European Integration (AEI) was initiated and created by Dr. Phil Wilkin, Social Sciences Bibliographer, University Library System, University of Pittsburgh, AEI Editor, and Dr. Michael Nentwich, Austrian Academy of Sciences, Institute of Technology Assessment, Vienna, Austria. Mr. Nentwich is a managing editor of the European Research Papers Archive, the only other online repository dedicated to the collection of full text materials on European integration.

Since the creation of the AEI in February 2003, the University Library System (ULS) has provided the technical and material support for the AEI. The task of designing and implementing the archive was undertaken by a team from the ULS Department of Information Systems including Timothy Deliyannides, Brian Gregg, Jeffrey Wisniewski and Demetrios Ioannides. The AEI is also supported by the European Union Center of Excellence and European Studies Center, University of Pittsburgh, and the European Union Studies Association (EUSA), housed at the University of Pittsburgh. Dr. Alberta Sbragia, former Director, European Union Center of Excellence and Center for European Studies, University of Pittsburgh, and current Vice Provost for Graduate Studies, University of Pittsburgh, serves as a consultant for AEI. Phil Wilkin administers all academic and intellectual aspects of the AEI.

Since Fall 2004, Barbara Sloan, formerly Head of Public Inquiries, Delegation of the European Commission to the US, Washington, DC, has been active in all phases of the development of the AEI-EU section of the AEI.

This site is powered by EPrints 3, free software developed by the University of Southampton.

Partners

ULS — University Library System

ERPA — European Research Papers Archive

European Union Center, University Center for International Studies, University of Pittsburgh

European Union Studies Association

ULS D-Scribe

This site is hosted by the University Library System of the University of Pittsburgh as part of its D-Scribe Digital Publishing Program

E-Prints

Archive of European Integration is powered by EPrints 3 which is developed by the School of Electronics and Computer Science at the University of Southampton. More information and software credits.

Share

Feeds

Atom

RSS 1.0

RSS 2.0

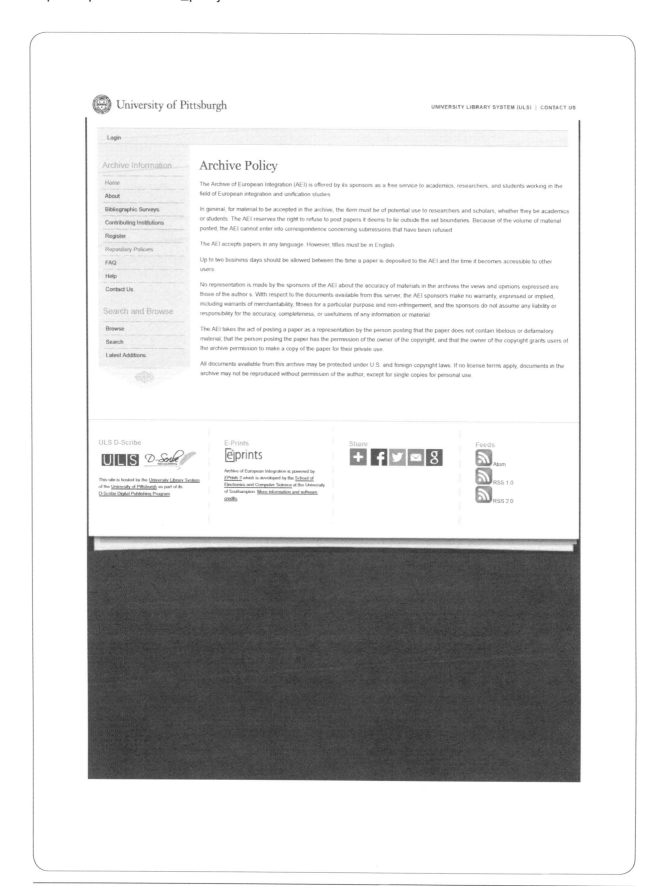

University of Pittsburgh

UNIVERSITY LIBRARY SYSTEM (ULS) | CONTACT US

Login

Archive Information

Home
About
Bibliographic Surveys
Contributing Institutions
Register
Repository Policies
FAQ
Help
Contact Us

Search and Browse

Browse
Search
Latest Additions

Archive Policy

The Archive of European Integration (AEI) is offered by its sponsors as a free service to academics, researchers, and students working in the field of European integration and unification studies

In general, for material to be accepted in the archive, the item must be of potential use to researchers and scholars, whether they be academics or students. The AEI reserves the right to refuse to post papers it deems to lie outside the set boundaries. Because of the volume of material posted, the AEI cannot enter into correspondence concerning submissions that have been refused.

The AEI accepts papers in any language. However, titles must be in English

Up to two business days should be allowed between the time a paper is deposited to the AEI and the time it becomes accessible to other users.

No representation is made by the sponsors of the AEI about the accuracy of materials in the archives the views and opinions expressed are those of the author s. With respect to the documents available from this server, the AEI sponsors make no warranty, expressed or implied, including warrants of merchantability, fitness for a particular purpose and non-infringement, and the sponsors do not assume any liability or responsibility for the accuracy, completeness, or usefulness of any information or material

The AEI takes the act of posting a paper as a representation by the person posting that the paper does not contain libelous or defamatory material, that the person posting the paper has the permission of the owner of the copyright; and that the owner of the copyright grants users of the archive permission to make a copy of the paper for their private use.

All documents available from this archive may be protected under U.S. and foreign copyright laws. If no license terms apply, documents in the archive may not be reproduced without permission of the author, except for single copies for personal use.

ULS D-Scribe

ULS D-Scribe

This title is hosted by the University Library System of the University of Pittsburgh as part of its D-Scribe Digital Publishing Program

E-Prints

[e]prints

Archive of European Integration is powered by EPrints 3 which is developed by the School of Electronics and Computer Science at the University of Southampton. More information and software credits.

Share

Feeds

Atom
RSS 1.0
RSS 2.0

tDAR

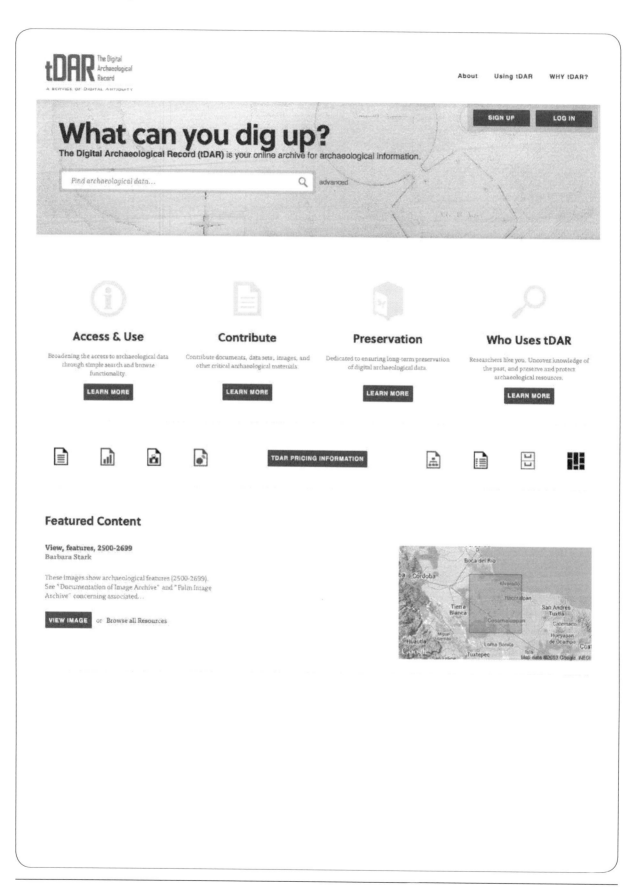

About

What is tDAR?

The Digital Archaeological Record (tDAR) is an international digital repository for the digital records of archaeological investigations. tDAR's use, development, and maintenance are governed by Digital Antiquity, an organization dedicated to ensuring the long-term preservation of irreplaceable archaeological data and to broadening the access to these data.

LEARN MORE

About Digital Antiquity

tDAR operates under the organizational umbrella of Digital Antiquity, a multi-institutional organization that has been explicitly designed to ensure the long-term financial, technical, and social sustainability of tDAR. Digital Antiquity is governed by an independent Board of Directors composed of four members with expertise in finance, law, not-for-profit organization administration, and information technology, plus individuals from the University of Arkansas, Arizona State University, the Pennsylvania State University, the SRI Foundation, Washington State University, and the University of York. Digital Antiquity's decision-making is supported by a distinguished external Professional Advisory Panel with representatives from all sectors of archaeology and from information science. Digital Antiquity is currently being incubated by Arizona State University. At the end of its initial development, the organization (and tDAR) may be established as a "stand-alone" not-for-profit organization or be incorporated into an appropriate non-profit, such as a professional association.

LEARN MORE

Supporters

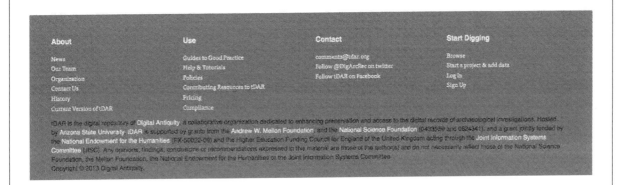

Using tDAR

tDAR is designed to serve the needs of a wide range of archaeologists, researchers, organizations, and institutions who use or manage archaeological resources.

Learn about different types of tDAR users and uses:

- Federal, State and Local Government Agencies
- Cultural Resource Management and Private Consulting Firms
- Academic Presses
- Academic Researchers and Organizations
- Educators

tDAR can assist users in:

- Managing a wide variety of archaeological information in one place.
- Organizing documents, data sets, and images.
- Downloading reports or bibliographies anywhere.
- Sharing current research materials with partners.
- Publishing data associated with articles and books.
- Protecting confidential materials.

- Preserving their legacy and contributing to the discipline.
- Guarding against data loss; preserving documents, data, and images.
- Fulfilling NSF, NEH, and other data management plan requirements.
- Complying with NHPA, ARPA, and 36 CFR 79.

Getting Started

- Help & Tutorials
- Policies & Procedures
- Contributing Resources
- Guides to Good Practice
- White Paper on Review, Redaction and Ingest of data into tDAR

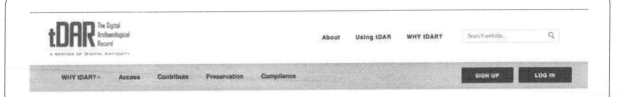

Find, create and share knowledge of our past and present.

Find & share research

As a repository for digital data, tDAR contains a vast amount of resources and tools that can enrich your ongoing research.

- Search our expansive database of documents, data sets, images and more.
- Integrate your data with data from other projects.
- Collaborate with other researchers

LEARN MORE

Preserve & protect data

The core mission of tDAR is to support better stewardship of the documents and data produced during research.

- Manage all of your archaeological data in one place.
- Organize your resources.
- Download reports or bibliographies.

LEARN MORE

Extend your classroom

As a discipline-specific archive of archaeological documents, tDAR is dedicated to the teaching of archaeology.

- Use reports, documents, data sets and images in classroom assignments and lectures.
- Find reports and grey literature from investigations from around the world.
- Compare different data sets and analyses.

LEARN MORE

Meet Your Legal Obligations

- ARPA
- NARA
- NHPA
- NSF
- NEH

Use tDAR to meet legal obligations to preserve and provide access to digital archaeological files, which mandate that data generated by federal agencies must be deposited in a repository capable of:

- Providing long-term digital curation;
- Ensuring preservation of the digital files; and
- Facilitating accessibility to qualified users.

LEARN MORE

Upload & Contribute to tDAR

In the Digital Archaeological Record (tDAR) you can deposit:

START NOW

Documents

PDF Documents (.pdf)   Text Documents (.txt)
Microsoft Word (.doc, .docx)
Rich Text Documents (.rtf)

Examples Reports of archaeological field investigations, articles presentations, field or lab notes, catalogs, dissertations or theses, collections and historical research, and historical documents about archaeological resources, research projects, and organizations

Images

Tagged Image File Format (.tiff, .tif)   Bitmap Image (.bmp)
Graphics Interchange Format (.gif)   PICT Image (.pict)
JPEG Image (.jpg, .jpeg)   Portable Network Graphics (.png)

Examples Images and illustrations of archaeological resources or related to archaeological investigations

Data Sets

Comma Separated Values (.csv)   Microsoft Excel (.xls, .xlsx)
Tab Separated Values (.tab)   Microsoft Access (.accdb, .mdb)

Examples Spreadsheets, databases, and coding sheets that describe archaeological data sets about artifacts, features, sites, or other archaeological phenomenon

Geospatial Data

Shapefiles   Geodatabases
Georectified images (GeoTIFF & Geo.JPG)

Examples Spatial Data about archaeological resources, e.g.: Maps

Virtual

Remote Sensing Files
3D Scans

Examples Data about archaeological resources collected by various sensors, e.g., GPS, GIS, Resistivity, GPR, and various sonar instruments

Confidentiality & Access Rights

Should you have sensitive materials, you have a number of options for protecting it in tDAR:

- Redaction of Lat/Long or coordinate information
- Limiting access to designated users
- Marking files as confidential
- Embargoing access to materials for 4 years

Once a file is marked as confidential or is embargoed, only users you specify can view or download files.

Things to Consider

As you collect your data and digital documents, keep these important things in mind:

- File naming conventions: Make it easy to distinguish different stages, drafts of documents, spreadsheets, databases, etc. Provide the most complete and recent set of data for long-term preservation and access.
- Back up files: Don't lose important data and have to recreate them.
- Protection: Separate potentially confidential information.
- Once marked as confidential or embargoed, only users you specify can view or download files.
- Consistency is key

What to put into tDAR:

- various kinds of documents, e.g., reports of archaeological field investigations, articles and presentations, field or lab notes, catalogs, dissertations or theses, collections and historical research, and historical documents and correspondence about archaeological resources, research projects, and organizations;
- spreadsheets, databases, and coding sheets that describe archaeological data sets about artifacts, features, sites, or other archaeological phenomenon;
- photographs, maps, and illustrations of archaeological resources or related to archaeological investigations; and
- data about archaeological resources collected by various sensors, e.g., GPS, GIS, Resistivity, GPR, and various sonar instruments.

MHHE Archive

Login

Minority Health and Health Equity Archive

Search & Browse

Simple Search

Advanced Search

Browse by Subject

Browse by Special Collection

Browse by Year

Information

Home

About the Archive

Archive Policy

Help

FAQ

Register

Contact Us

Welcome to The Minority Health and Health Equity Archive, an electronic archive for digital resource materials in the fields of minority health and health disparities research and policy. It is offered as a no-charge resource to the public, academic scholars and health science researchers interested in the elimination of racial and ethnic health disparities.

The goal of the Archive is to advance the use of new digital technologies to promote trans-disciplinary scholarship on race, ethnicity and disparities research designed to achieve health equity. The Archive will help facilitate the rapid dissemination of new work in the professional literature as well as the gray literature including, but not limited to, historical documents, government resources, teaching tools and commentary. Authors who wish to post papers to the Archive should first consult the Archive Policy.

The archive offers a category called "Browse By Subject" intended as a convenience to those searching for information regarding specific topical areas. Additionally, this method offers a convenient way for you to review our content "at a glance", as you evaluate your own documents for contribution as relevant to the current structure of the archive.

Currently, our archive contents include materials which have been listed in the following subject domains:

- Government Publications (including reports and publications from the National Institutes of Health, State Departments of Public Health, the US Department of Health and Human Services, and the national Office of Minority Health).

- Health (including specific health areas such as Disparities, Global Health, Health Equity, Access To Healthcare, Access To Healthy Foods, Bioethics, Nutrition, Policy, and Prenatal and Pediatric Health

- Public Health (including material on specific chronic illnesses and health risk factors such as Cancer,Cardiovascular Disease,Diabetes, HIV/Aids,Hypertension,Mental Health,Obesity,Health Risk Factors.

- Practice (interventions, outreach, and service)

- Research (Capacity Development, Genetics, methodologies, studies)

- Teaching (Risk Management, Community Redevelopment, methods)

Posting to this area is restricted to those registered as users. All visitors of the Archive may become a registered user by going to the registered users area and completing the online registration form. All content posted to the archive can be read by all users of the archive, whether or not they become registered users.

Sponsored by

- The Maryland Center for Health Equity, School of Public Health, University of Maryland College Park
- University Library System, University of Pittsburgh

Statistics

- There are currently **2585** articles available in this archive.

Minority Health and Health Equity Archive supports OAI 2.0 with a base URL of http://health-equity.pitt.edu/cgi/oai2

University of Pittsburgh

ULS D-Scribe

This site is hosted by the University

UNIVERSITY OF MARYLAND
CENTER FOR HEALTH EQUITY

Share

Feeds

Atom   RSS 1.0

RSS 2.0

Login

About the Archive

Search & Browse

Simple Search

Advanced Search

Browse by Subject

Browse by Special Collection

Browse by Year

Information

Home

About the Archive

Archive Policy

Help

FAQ

Register

Contact Us

History

The Minority Health and Health Equity Archive was originally founded in 2004 as the Minority Health Archive by Dr. Stephen B. Thomas in collaboration with the Center for Minority Health and the University Library System at the University of Pittsburgh to serve as an online repository of print and electronic media related to the health of the four nationally recognized minority groups in the United States: African American/Black, Native American, Hispanic/Latino, and Asian American/Pacific Islander (See the NIH policy on reporting race and ethnicity data for subjects in clinical research, NOTICE NOT-OD-01-053).

Since its creation, the University Library System, University of Pittsburgh (ULS) has provided technical and material support for the Minority Health and Health Equity Archive in its ongoing commitment to free and open access to scholarly research material. In 2011, the editorship of the Archive moved from the University of Pittsburgh's Center for Minority Health to the University of Maryland Center for Health Equity, established November 2010 under the direction of Dr. Stephen B. Thomas. The Archive continues to be hosted by the University Library System, University of Pittsburgh as part of its part of its D-Scribe Digital Publishing program.

Contents of the Minority Health and Health Equity Archive

The Minority Health and Health Equity Archive has a goal to be the primary repository and archive for all materials related to minority health. Therefore, materials submitted to the Minority Health and Health Equity Archive must deal with or relate to the health of the minority racial/ethnic groups in the United States (Black/African American, Native American, Native Hawaiian, Latino/Hispanic, and Asian American/Pacific Islander). The materials submitted can be about the general health, current research involving, or health disparities among any of these particular groups as well as materials related to the major contributors and contributions to the field of minority health. Materials can include journal articles, web-based materials, government documents, books, book chapters, conference proceedings, conference papers, course outlines, events/presentations, images, pre-prints,theses/dissertations, and other materials relevant to our goal.

Administration and Support

The Minority Health and Health Equity Archive is hosted by the University Library System, University of Pittsburgh., as part of its D-Scribe Digital Publishing program

This site is powered by EPrints 3, free software developed by the University of Southampton.

University of Pittsburgh

ULS D-Scribe

This site is hosted by the University Library System of the University of Pittsburgh as part of its D-Scribe Digital Publishing Program

UNIVERSITY OF MARYLAND
CENTER FOR HEALTH EQUITY

Share

Feeds

Atom   RSS 1.0

RSS 2.0

Login

Search & Browse

Simple Search

Advanced Search

Browse by Subject

Browse by Special Collection

Browse by Year

Information

Home

About the Archive

Archive Policy

Help

FAQ

Register

Contact Us

Policies

Metadata Policy

for information describing items in the repository

1. Anyone may access the metadata free of charge.
2. The metadata may be re-used in any medium without prior permission for not-for-profit purposes and re-sold commercially provided the OAI Identifier or a link to the original metadata record are given.

Data Policy

for full-text and other full data items

1. Anyone may access full items free of charge.
2. No full-item re-use policy defined. Assume no rights at all have been granted.

Content Policy

for types of document & data set held

1. This is a multi-institution subject-based repository.
2. No content policy defined.

Submission Policy

concerning depositors, quality & copyright

1. Items may only be deposited by accredited members of the subject community
2. Eligible depositors must deposit bibliographic metadata for all their publications.
3. The administrator only vets items for relevance to the scope of Minority Health and Health Equity Archive, and the exclusion of spam
4. The validity and authenticity of the content of submissions is the sole responsibility of the depositor.
5. No embargo policy defined.
6. Any copyright violations are entirely the responsibility of the authors/depositors.
7. If Minority Health and Health Equity Archive receives proof of copyright violation, the relevant item will be removed immediately.
8. For more information see webpage: http://health-equity.pitt.edu/policy.html

Preservation Policy

1. Items will be retained indefinitely.
2. Minority Health and Health Equity Archive will try to ensure continued readability and accessibility.
   - It may not be possible to guarantee the readability of some unusual file formats.
3. Minority Health and Health Equity Archive regularly backs up its files according to current best practice.
4. Items may not normally be removed from Minority Health and Health Equity Archive.
5. Acceptable reasons for withdrawal include:
   - Proven copyright violation or plagiarism
   - Legal requirements and proven violations
   - National Security
   - Falsified research
6. Withdrawn items are not deleted *per se*, but are removed from public view.
7. Withdrawn items' identifiers/URLs are retained indefinitely.
8. URLs will continue to point to 'tombstone' citations, to avoid broken links and to retain item histories.
9. The metadata of withdrawn items will not be searchable.
10. *Errata* and *corrigenda* lists may be included with the original record if required.
11. If necessary, an updated version may be deposited.
12. No closure policy defined.
13. For more information see webpage: http://health-equity.pitt.edu/policy.html

University of Pittsburgh

ULS D-Scribe

This site is hosted by the University

UNIVERSITY OF MARYLAND
CENTER FOR HEALTH EQUITY

Share

Feeds

Atom   RSS 1.0

RSS 2.0

Login

Frequently Asked Questions

Search & Browse

Simple Search
Advanced Search
Browse by Subject
Browse by Special Collection
Browse by Year

Information

Home
About the Archive
Archive Policy
Help
FAQ
Register
Contact Us

What is the Minority Health Archive?

The Minority Health Archive, created in collaboration with the Center for Minority Health and the University Library System at the University of Pittsburgh , is an online repository of various print and/or electronic media related to the health of the four nationally recognized racial groups (Blacks/African Americans, Native Americans, Hispanics/Latinos, and Asian Americans/Pacific Islanders). The Minority Health Archive provides the opportunity to not only research and gather various documents in a variety of subject areas, but also a resource to deposit other related materials not already posted to the archive.

Who has access to the Minority Health Archive?

Anyone can access the information in the archive. However, registration is required if one wants to submit resources to be posted to the archive, or receive automatic e-mails notifying you of new content in the Archive. To register, from the home page, http://minority-health.pitt.edu, click on the Register link in the top menu bar. Follow the instructions to fill out the online registration form. You will receive a confirmation e-mail with a link to follow in order to finalize the registration process.

What kind of information can be included in the Archive?

Materials submitted to the Minority Health Archive must deal with or relate to the health of the minority racial/ethnic groups in the United States (Black/African American, Native American, Native Hawaiian, Latino/Hispanic, and Asian American/Pacific Islander). The materials submitted can be about the general health, current research involving, or health disparities among any of these particular groups as well as materials related to the major contributors and contributions to the field of minority health.

Materials can include journal articles, web-based materials, government documents, books, book chapters, conference proceedings, conference papers, course outlines, events/presentations, images, pre-prints, theses/dissertations, and other materials relevant to our goal.

Can I submit an article or other document to the Archive? If so, how?

Yes any registered user can submit new documents to the Archive . In order to post a resource, registration is required. To register, from the home page, http://minority-health.pitt.edu, click on the Register link in the top menu bar. Follow the instructions to fill out the online registration form. You will receive a confirmation e-mail with a link to follow in order to finalize the registration process.

To post a resource to the archive, click on the Registered Users Area link. A window will open prompting you to sign in with a user name and password. If you have not already registered, click on Cancel and then click on the Register link on the main page. Follow steps mentioned above. Once you have signed in, you will be taken to your user area homepage, which is denoted with your name at the top of the page. Several item s appear in your workspace. All links have descriptions below them for you to understand each purpose. You will also find a blank box entitled , Documents in your Workspace, with several buttons below it. This box holds all of the documents that you are working on, but have not submit ted. Below the Documents in your Workspace box, there is a section called Pending Items. In this area, those documents that you have submitted for approval will appear here until they has been approved or denied.

To begin posting a new resource, click the New button. You will then be asked to choose the type of media you are posting. Most are self explanatory, but Journal (Paginated) is the form for journal articles. If the choices available do not best describe the type of media you want to post choose Other. Each type presents a form specific to citation format for that type of media. All have a specific set of required information needed in order to proceed. If you find that you do not have any of the required information, try Other. Other offers all the options for a ll of the forms with less required information. Once you have chosen a type, then click the Next button. (Note: If you start a new deposit and then cancel, the deposit will appear in your Documents in your Workspace box as Untitled with a number (i.e., Untitled 134). You can choose t o reuse it by highlighting the Untitled document and then clicking Edit or you can delete it by highlighting the Untitled document and clicking delete.) After you click the Next button, you will be taken to the Bibliographic Information page. Follow directions and be sure to complete all required fields indicated with a red asterisk (*). When you have completed this form, then click the Next button.

The following page is the Document Information page. Here choose the type of electronic format of your document/resource. For Word or any other standard text documents choose ASCII. You may also offer an additional brief description of the format in the text box below the choices. Th en click the Next button. You will then be taken to the Document File Upload page. There, choose what method you would like to use to upload, and then choose how many uploads you will be making. (Typically, there will only be one uploaded file.) Once you have indicated the method and the number to upload, click the Upload button.

The following page will be Document File Upload. Here it will show you what you have just uploaded and allow you to upload another document. You are also able to preview what you uploaded before proceeding to the next step. If all is correct and you are finished, then click the Finished button. Now you will be taken to the Document Storage Formats page which will show you what format of the document you just uploaded and h ow many. Here you may again add a document or continue by clicking the Next button.

The final step in the process of submitting a document or resource is to verify all the information in the deposit you just made. You will see two versions of how your deposit will appear. The first version (in a gray box) is how it will appear in the archive upon approval. The second version is how it will appear to the editorial staff. Double check your deposit for grammatical errors and missing information. If you need to make any changes just click the Back button until you reach the page that you need to make the edit. If you want to wait to make your deposit, click the Deposit EPrint Later button. This button will place the deposit in your workspace for later action. If all is complete and you a re ready to submit, click the Deposit EPrint Now button. This will take you to a Thank You page which gives you a brief description of the approval process. From this page there is a link that will take you back to your workspace.

For materials that have been submitted for posting to the archive, there may be a 2-3 week evaluation period to verify permissions related to the source before posting to the archive.

Is the Minority Health Archive a searchable database?

Yes.

To Search From the home page http://minority-health.pitt.edu, choose any of the hyperlinks indicating Sear ch. You may perform either a simple or advanced search. The simple search allows you to search by title/keyword, author(s)/editor(s), or year. The advanced search allows you to search the same categories as simple search as well as by subject, Eprint Type (book, journal (paginated)-journal article, conference proceedings, etc), conference, department, and publication. You can also choose how you want the result to appear by using the drop down menu.

To Browse From the home page http://minority-health.pitt.edu, choose any of the hyperlinks indicating Browse. One may browse by subject (i.e., research, health, etc), by year, or the Pioneer Collections. Just click on the links that are of interest to you. You can also choose how you want the result to appear by using the drop down menu. (The Pioneer Collection, which will recognize major pioneers in the field of minority health, is currently under development; therefore no information is available on any of these links. We expect for this to be fully open by Summer 2006.)

How do I search for a particular author, topic, or journal?

From the home page http://minority-health.pitt.edu, choose any of the hyperlinks indicating Sear ch. You may perform either a simple or advanced search. The simple search allows you to search by title/keyword, author(s)/editor(s), or year. The advanced search allows you to search the same categories as simple search as well as by subject, Eprint Type (book, journal (paginated)-journal article, conference proceedings, etc), conference, department, and publication. You can also choose how you want the result to appear b y using the drop down menu.

What kinds of information can I submit to the archive?

Materials submitted to the Minority Health Archive must deal with or relate to the health of the minority racial/ethnic groups in the United States (Black/African American, Native American, Native Hawaiian, Latino/Hispanic, and Asian American/Pacific Islander). The materials submitted can be about the general health, current research involving, or health disparities among any of these particular groups as well as materials related to the major contributors and contributions to the field of minority health.

Materials can include journal articles, web-based materials, government documents, books, book chapters, conference proceedings, conference papers, course outlines, events/presentations, images, pre-prints, theses/dissertations, and other materials relevant to our goal.

How does the archive differ from a journal?

A journal publishes material that has passed scrutiny by referees and has been edited by the editorial staff to bring it to the journal standards. The archive does not referee postings and does not edit them. The archive merely filters minimally to assure relevance to philosophy of science.

May we submit material to the archive that has appeared elsewhere? The archive does not require or expect that material has not appeared elsewhere. However, if it has appeared elsewhere, the author must determine whether copyright was transferred from the author and whether the copyright agreement allows posting on the archive. While we do not object to duplication, the other source may.

Do I lose copyright privileges when I submit a document to the archive?

No. Works contributed to the archive remain fully protected by US and other copyright laws. Under US copyright law, your work is under copyright protection the moment it is created and fixed in a tangible form. Even though the copyright for your work may not be registered, you are encouraged to assert your copyright on the title page of your work. For more information, see http://www.copyright.gov.

Will posting on the archive affect subsequent attempts to publish in a journal?

This is a matter for the individual journals to decide. These policies are in flux with the trend towards greater tolerance.

If I post a preprint on the archive and then publish it in a journal or volume, can I leave the preprint on the archive?

Individual journal policies vary on this question. Whatever the policy, the authoritative document is the copyright agreement you sign with the publisher. If that agreement requires you to remove the posted preprint, you should by notifying us at minority-health@library.pitt.edu.

May I remove a preprint once it is posted?

Yes. Papers can be removed. Unfortunately the archive does not allow you to remove papers automatically. Removal is initiated with a removal request, accessible through the links "Deposit Papers" --> "Review your documents in the archive". Archive staff will then remove the paper as quickly as possible, typically within one business day. All requests for removal will be honored, although we encourage you to leave preprints posted for stability of the archive's contents.

Is there any special connection between the archive and any other journals?

The archive is sponsored solely by the University of Pittsburgh Center for Minority Health, which is an academic center in the Graduate School of Public Health. The archive is not affiliated with any journal.

How long does it take after a preprint is deposited with the archive for the preprint to become available to the public?

Allow until the end of the next business day following the day the deposit is made. When a preprint is deposited, it immediately gets sent to our "submission buffer" where a staff member does a quick routine check of the preprint's suitability for Minority Health Archive. The paper i s then publicly accessible via a search, though it may not appear immediately in the "browse tree" which is updated routinely.

Can I link to the Minority Health Archive from my Website?

Yes, we encourage linkages to our site. Use this URL for the link: http://minority-health.pitt.edu

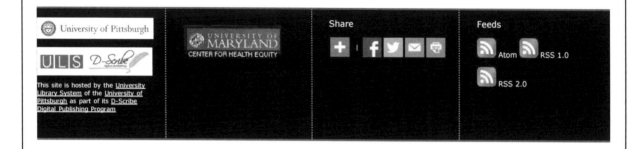

SELECTED RESOURCES

General Articles about Disciplinary Repositories

Adamick, Jessica, and Rebecca Reznik-Zellen. "Trends in Large-scale Subject Repositories." *D-Lib Magazine* 16, no. 11/12 (2010). http://dx.doi.org/10.1045/november2010-adamick

Adamick, Jessica, and Rebecca Reznik-Zellen. "Representation and Recognition of Subject Repositories." *D-Lib Magazine* 16, no. 9/10 (2010). http://dx.doi.org/10.1045/september2010-adamick

Armbruster, Chris, and Laurent Romary. "Comparing Repository Types. Challenges and Barriers for Subject-based Repositories, Research Repositories, National Repository Systems and Institutional Repositories in Serving Scholarly Communication." *arXiv preprint arXiv:1003.4187* (2010). http://arxiv.org/ftp/arxiv/papers/1005/1005.0839.pdf

Bjork, Bo-Christer. "Open Access Subject Repositories: An Overview." Journal of the American Society for Information Science and Technology Early View (2013). http://dx.doi.org/10.1002/asi.23021

Darby, Robert, Catherine Jones, Linda Gilbert, and Simon Lambert. "Increasing the Productivity of Interactions Between Subject and Institutional Repositories." *New Review of Information Networking* 14, no. 2 (2009): 117–35. http://dx.doi.org/10.1080/13614570903359381

Qing, Feng, and Huang Ruhua. "Evaluating the Usability of Discipline Repositories." *Proceedings of 2008 IEEE International Symposium on IT in Medicine and Education.* 385–90. IEEE, 2008. http://dx.doi.org/10.1109/ITME.2008.4743892

Interuniversity Consortium for Political and Social Research. *Sustaining Domain Repositories for Digital Data: A Call for Change from an Interdisciplinary Working Group of Domain Repositories.* 2013. http://www.icpsr.umich.edu/files/ICPSR/pdf/DomainRepositoriesCTA16Sep2013.pdf

Thomas, Sarah E. "Publishing Solutions for Contemporary Scholars: The Library as Innovator and Partner." *Library Hi Tech* 24, no. 4 (2006): 563–73. http://dx.doi.org/10.1108/07378830610715428

Xia, Jingfeng. "A Comparison of Subject and Institutional Repositories in Self-Archiving Practices." *The Journal of Academic Librarianship* 34, no. 6 (2008): 489–95. http://dx.doi.org/10.1016/j.acalib.2008.09.016

Xia, Jingfeng. "Disciplinary Repositories in the Social Sciences." In *Aslib Proceedings* 59, no. 6 (2007): 528–38. http://dx.doi.org/10.1108/00012530710839605

Information about the Case Study Disciplinary Repositories

AgEcon Search

Kelly, Julie, and Louise Letnes. "AgEcon Search: A Case Study on the Differences Between Operating a Subject Repository and an Institutional Repository." *JoDI: Journal of Digital Information* 12, no. 2 (2011). http://journals.tdl.org/jodi/index.php/jodi/article/view/733/639

Kelly, Julie, and Louise Letnes. "Managing the Grey Literature of a Discipline Through Collaboration: AgEcon Search." *Resource Sharing & Information Networks* 18, no. 1–2 (2006): 157–66. http://dx.doi.org/10.1300/J121v18n01_12

Letnes, Louise, and Julie Kelly. "AgEcon Search: Expanding the Distribution of Current Literature in One Subdiscipline of Agriculture." *Agricultural Information Worldwide* 1, no. 1 (2008): 29. http://journals.sfu.ca/iaald/index.php/aginfo/article/view/10/9

Letnes, Louise, and Julie Kelly. "AgEcon Search: History and Future of a Collaborative Subject Repository." *Journal of Agricultural & Food Information* 9, no. 4 (2008): 324–28. http://dx.doi.org/10.1080/10496500802483254

Letnes, Louise, and Julie Kelly. "AgEcon Search: Partners Build a Web Resource." *Issues in Science & Technology Librarianship* 34 (2002). http://istl.org/02-spring/article3.html

Rodkewich, Patricia, and Louise Letnes. "AgEcon Search: Research in Agricultural Economics–Working Papers on the Internet." *Journal of Agricultural & Food Information* 3, no. 2 (1996): 23–29. http://dx.doi.org/10.1300/J108V03N02_04

PubMed Central®

Fischel, Martha, and Carol J. Myers. "The PubMed Central Archive and the Back Issue Scanning Project." *Journal of Interlibrary Loan, Document Delivery & Electronic Reserve* 17, no. 3 (2007): 109–16. http://dx.doi.org/10.1300/J474v17n03_14

Homan, J. Michael, and Linda A. Watson. "STM Publishing Meets NIH Digital Archive: Librarian Service on the PubMed Central National Advisory Committee." *Reference Services Review* 32, no. 1 (2004): 83–88. http://dx.doi.org/10.1108/00907320410519504

Kiley, Robert. "The Medical Journals Back-Files Digitization Project and Open Access." *Serials* 19, no. 2 (2006): 95–102. http://dx.doi.org/10.1629/1995

Kling, R., Spector, L. B., and Fortuna, J. "The Real Stakes of Virtual Publishing: The Transformation of E-Biomed Into PubMed Central." *Journal of the American Society for Information Science and Technology* 55, no. 2 (2004): 127–48. http://dx.doi.org/10.1002/asi.10352

Smith, Kent, and Ed Sequeira. "Linking at the US National Library of Medicine." *Learned Publishing* 14 no. 1 (2001): 23–28. http://dx.doi.org/10.1087/09531510125100232

HABRI Central

Knowledge Base
https://habricentral.org/kb/

InterNano

Reznik-Zellen, Rebecca, and Jessica Adamick. "Supporting Virtual Communities Through Disciplinary Repository Development." *Library Hi Tech* 30, no. 2 (2012): 275–90. http://dx.doi.org/10.1108/07378831211239951

Dryad

Beagrie, Neil, Lorraine Eakin-Richards, and Todd Vision. "Business Models and Cost Estimation: Dryad Repository Case Study." In *iPres2010. Proceedings of the 7th International Conference on Preservation of Digital Objects*. (2010): 365–70. http://www.ifs.tuwien.ac.at/dp/ipres2010)/papers/beagrie-37.pdf

Carrier, Sarah. "The Dryad Repository Application Profile: Process, Development, and Refinement." Master's Thesis, University of North Carolina at Chapel Hill, 2008. http://www.ils.unc.edu/MSpapers/3355.pdf

Greenberg, Jane. "Theoretical Considerations of Lifecycle Modeling: An Analysis of the Dryad Repository Demonstrating Automatic Metadata Propagation, Inheritance, and Value System Adoption." *Cataloging & Classification Quarterly* 47, no. 3–4 (2009): 380–402. http://dx.doi.org/10.1080/01639370902737547

Greenberg, Jane, Hollie C. White, Sarah Carrier, and Ryan Scherle. "A Metadata Best Practice for a Scientific Data Repository." *Journal of Library Metadata* 9, no. 3/4 (2009): 194–212. http://dx.doi.org/10.1080/19386380903405090

Luyten, Bram, Mark Diggory, and Peggy Schaeffer. "Subject Repositories for Research Data: The Dryad Approach." Presented at the *European Library Automation Group (ELAG) Annual Conference*, Palma de Mallorca, Spain, May 16–18, 2012. https://atmire.com/dspace-labs3/bitstream/handle/123456789/11845/ELAG-DRYAD-ATMIRE-FINAL.pdf?sequence=1

Vision, Todd. "The Dryad Digital Repository: Published Evolutionary Data as Part of the Greater Data Ecosystem." *Nature Precedings* (2010). http://dx.doi.org/10101/npre.2010.4595.1

White, Hollie, Sarah Carrier, Abbey Thompson, Jane Greenberg, and Ryan Scherle. "The Dryad Data Repository: A Singapore Framework Metadata Architecture in a DSpace Environment." In *Proceedings of the International Conference on Dublin Core and Metadata Applications 2008*. (2008): 157. http://edoc.hu-berlin.de/conferences/dc-2008/white-hollie-157/PDF/white.pdf

Dryad Bylaws
http://wiki.datadryad.org/wg/dryad/images/2/24/DryadByLaws_v5.pdf

Board of Directors Manual and Best Practices
http://wiki.datadryad.org/wg/dryad/images/a/a3/BoardManual.pdf#page=2

Business Plan and Sustainability
http://wiki.datadryad.org/Business_Plan_and_Sustainability

Archive of European Integration (AEI)

Wilkin, Phil. "The Archive of European Integration: Resources for European Law." *Legal Information Management* 9, no. 2 (2009): 112–16. http://dx.doi.org/10.1017/S1472669609000280

The Digital Archaeological Record (tDAR)

Kansa, Eric C., Sarah Whitcher Kansa, Francis P. McManamon, Keith W. Kintigh, Adam Brin, and Andrea Vianello. "Digital Antiquity and the Digital Archaeological Record (tDAR): Broadening Access and Ensuring Long-Term Preservation for Digital Archaeological Data." *The CSA Newsletter* XXIII, no. 2 (2010). http://csanet.org/newsletter/fall10/nlf1002.html

Kintigh, Keith W., and Jeffrey H. Altschul. "Sustaining the Digital Archaeological Record." *Heritage Management* 3, no. 2 (2010): 264–74. http://www.tdar.org/wp-uploads/www.digitalantiquity. org/2011/01/20110127-Kintigh-Altschul-Forum-on-Sustaining-the-Digital-Archaeological-Record-from-Heritage-Management.pdf

Spielmann, Katherine A., and Keith W. Kintigh. "The Digital Archaeological Record: The Potentials of Archaeozoological Data Integration Through tDAR" *SAA Archaeological Record* (2011). http:// alexandriaarchive.org/bonecommons/archive/files/spielmann_kintigh_icaz_saa_jan2011_8025c1e7b5. pdf

tDAR Data Dictionary
https://dev.tdar.org/confluence/display/TDAR/Data+Dictionary

History
http://www.tdar.org/about/history/

Policies
http://www.tdar.org/about/policies/

Pricing
http://www.tdar.org/about/pricing/

Note: All URLs accessed 11/18/13.

DATE DUE

GAYLORD

PRINTED IN U.S.A.